Dedications

To my cousin Taneasha, who used to lock me up but turned out to be my Emancipator from the Hades where I lived for years.

To my cousin Jamie, who always had my back.
To all my aunts, who stood behind me.

To Barbara for all the good years we shared.
To Scotty for all the hugs and encouragement she gave.
To Teri Catlin, who sings about it straight to my soul.
To Lee Jameson-Krampp for all of the toiling he did.

and

To April, who taught me true friendship, understanding, and acceptance…who relived it all with me and will help me write the exciting new chapters in my life.

I love you all and thank you!
Love
Kathryn Harriet Muhammad

D1399985

T.O.I.L.

(Triumph Over Innocence Lost)

Toil

noun \ ˈtȯi(-ə)l\

struggle, battle, laborious effort, long strenuous fatiguing labor

By

Kathryn Muhammad And April L. Braun

Prologue

Innocence: in·no·cence \ in – ə – səns \
Noun: lack of guile or corruption, purity

Tragedy: trag·e·dy \ tra – j ə – dē \
Noun: a disastrous event, calamity

Triumph: tri·umph \ trī – əm(ph) \
Noun: the joy or exultation of victory or success

Have you experienced episodes in your life that haunt you day and night, consciously and unconsciously, to the exclusion of all else? Have you ever been abused or raped? Have you awakened in a hospital after you had tried to wake up in heaven? Have you ever felt responsible for the death of someone else? Have you ever been hunted by other human beings? If you have, then you can relate strongly to this story. You will know how hard it can be to struggle to survive after such events. You will know what it means to TOIL!

My name is Kathryn Harriet Muhammad, and my life has been one bizarre string of events after another. I have experienced all of the things above; I have struggled, I've been knocked down, I've stumbled and fallen down. Yet I didn't stay down. I have repeatedly picked myself back up and staggered forward. I have not only survived; I have triumphed.

I started life as a preemie and was raised by a poor single mom after the divorce of my parents. Nevertheless, I was a happy child. But I gained a stepfather who ended up being a monster. I endured years of psychological and sexual abuse from him. I tried repeatedly to die, but my indomitable innermost will to survive drove me to not only live but to excel.

I broke away from my horrible past, strove to make a difference in children's lives, and succeeded spectacularly. That is, until tragedy struck — tragedy that blindsided me and destroyed my life. I was indirectly responsible for the death of a little girl. I became front-page news. I was hunted day and night by the press. Nothing in my life was sacred anymore. I lost everything I held dear. I would never be trusted again.

That is, until NBC's *Dateline* showed up at my door intending to make *me* into a monster. Instead, when I opened up my heart and bared my soul to them, they listened; they felt my pain. *Dateline* became my champion and not my destroyer. The vindication that NBC's investigation brought eased my soul, but it came too late to repair my crumbling empire. Nevertheless, my exoneration was complete. Now I could move forward with my life and my dream to help children by creating safety products and training videos, and equally important, if not more so, through the written expression of my life experiences.

While I march on my new journey, I hope to flourish again with the wounds of my past finally healed. As I travel down this jagged and treacherous path, I reflect on my life and what I have lost. Yet, my determination is to excel instead of just to survive. I think of all the people who, along with me, suffered so, and I ponder what we all once had but lost along the way. I believe it was our innocence.

When I think of innocence, my thoughts frequently center on the purity and the naivety of a child and the simplistic way children perceive the world around them, trusting everyone in their sphere to not only provide for their wants and needs, but frankly expecting everyone who is responsible for their happiness to love and to protect them.

Conversely, when I think of lost innocence, my thoughts shy away from the possibility that a child might be affected. I do not want to acknowledge the disasters that can befall innocent children, especially tragedies caused by the malice or neglect of the very people expected to care for them. I don't really like to think of these things—and for good reason. They remind me too much of what happened to me.

I truly believe that we are all born innocent and that most of us endeavor to live our adult lives absent of guile. Sometimes, though, our innocence is taken from us by others. We can live without it; however, when it's gone, I think it usually (and unfortunately) is replaced by guilt.

This is a story about two beautiful children who define the way I think of lost innocence. It is about my own tragic loss and another's life taken, about how I raised myself from the abysmal childhood I was forced to endure and how I strove to become an exemplary adult committed to the protection and love of the children entrusted to me. And it is about my little Haile Brockington, who did not survive to enjoy the pleasures or to experience the toils of life, simply because of the neglect of duty by the very adults who were expected to care for her.

Our lives, mine and Haile's, are conjoined forever by the thoughtless tragedy that occurred on August 5, 2010. The events of that August day disastrously affected us both and shattered the lives of many of the people around us. Haile died that cataclysmic day. The repercussions reached far and wide, engulfing the truly innocent and transforming them forever into the psychologically guilty.

1. Introduction to Me

"Who am I?" This is the extremely torturous question my therapist recently posed to me. It is brutal because I have lived in a quandary nearly my entire existence long, pondering who I am and what my role in life is supposed to be.

Most recently, I was Katie, of Katie's Kids Learning Center. It was a nickname given me as a child, and I kept it through the seven years I owned and operated my four pre-schools. Now I cannot stand to hear my abbreviated name spoken, because it doesn't mean much without my kids.

I tried to give everything I never had to the children entrusted to me. I wanted them to be able to escape from the hard lives they lived at home. I wanted them to be able to dream big and reach for the stars, like I had. I lived through those kids. Their hopes and dreams became mine. Helping them achieve their desires, while they lived a tough day-to-day life, was a way for me to give something back to the community, to the moms and dads who'd placed their children in my care. I wanted to save all of these little ones and to help them prepare to make the world a better place. It was the means by which I could escape from my own horrible past. I wouldn't want that particular history to repeat itself for anyone. These kids saved my life by keeping me so busy that I

1

could forget my own demons. This was my mission in life. This was who I was. This was once my answer to the question, "Who am I?"

I lost it all because Haile died! I lost my kids! Somehow, through everything, I also lost myself. I had lived, breathed, and dreamed the children. I was supposed to. Through my schools, I was trusted to take care of them and prepare them for life. I took my job seriously, and I took it to heart.

So, who am I, as I was asked? While I still don't know the answer, I do know that I am determined to find out and make the rest of my journey a forceful one in the protection of children.

The beginning of my life was not so straightforward.

I was born in Boston, Massachusetts, as Kathryn Harriet Muhammad on March 6, 1980, to a racially and religiously diverse couple: Thomasina Thompson and Lawrence Muhammad. I was a mix of black, French, American Indian, white, and a few other strains of humanity: rather a mutt, who could not be classified even at birth. What race box could my parents check for me? Is there one for "all of the above?" I doubt it. Having both a Christian and a Muslim parent didn't help one bit.

My mother became pregnant with me at seventeen years old, and I believe she married my father because of it. My maternal grandmother died very unexpectedly when my mother was only eight months along with me. The trauma of losing her mother sent my mom into premature labor, and my battle for life began. It was my first struggle to survive and probably the easiest, but definitely not the last.

Being severely underweight and jaundiced, I didn't get to go home with my parents right away. I spent two months in the hospital, with my indomitable will to live coming to the forefront. Starting life in the care of nurses, since Mom had to go back to work, I wasn't breast-fed or cuddled much, and I sometimes wonder if the lasting bond that should have been forged with my mother at that point broke down then instead.

When I finally was brought home, it was not into the perfect family life, as I learned later. My mother was extremely depressed, and my father was battling his own psychological demons. Even so, it was home—for a short while, anyway.

My mom said I learned to walk really early—by the age of nine months—because my dad could be loud and obnoxious, and I'd want to get away from his crazy antics. I don't remember him from when he lived with us at all. I was just too young. My father left some indelible impressions upon me though, which my mom would later explain when I grew older.

For instance, I was terrified of my grandfather's cigarette lighter. Whenever he'd light up, I'd go scurrying from the room like a terrified rabbit with the hounds of hell on its tail. My mom explained that once when I was a toddler, Dad caught me with a lighter. He lit it up, held the flame for a moment, and then placed my finger against the hot metal at the top. Talk about a cure for ever wanting to play with fire. It was a brutal lesson, and boy, did it work.

I also wouldn't go near a stove when anyone was cooking. Well, my mom explained that one evening, Dad had been chasing me around for a tickle fight and I had rammed into her just as she was turning from the stove with a pot of boiling soup. The big scar on my right arm marks where that blistering liquid landed and scorched the top few layers of skin right off my tender young body.

My mom told me that she and my father fought a great deal. Her depression and his psychological issues combined to overpower the relationship, leading to the demise of the marriage. My parents divorced when I was only two.

So there I was, with a single mother who was poor, but who made me feel loved and cherished as the nucleus of her being. She would read to me for hours with her honeyed voice, her dark chocolate eyes glittering in the lamplight, her soft black hair stroking the collar of her bathrobe when she turned her head. I'd be enthralled by the stories and her presentation of them. I'd be mesmerized by the movement of her rose-colored lips as she spoke and would wait in excited anticipation for her lovely smile to blossom at something humorous in a story. She was beautiful, and she was all mine.

As I reached pre-school age, she could not afford to send me to an accredited pre-school, so I stayed in a family daycare while she worked long hours. It was a rowdy bunch of scruffy little kids. We were all stuffed into one room on the bottom floor of some three-story house, where we played and took hated naps. I was happy enough, though, because the kids were all just like me.

We'd clatter around on the hardwood floors, our shouts and cries echoing through the house. The only time we were allowed outside was when we'd go for a walk. The day-care was located in a lower-middle-class neighborhood with rows of three-story buildings huddled together, crowding the street. The owner would keep us under control by making us hang onto a rope. We'd look like a scraggly bunch of ducklings lined up behind their waddling mother. I always wondered what would happen if I let go of the rope, but was too timid to find out. I worried that I'd be snatched by some bad guy or get gobbled up by the ominous shadows cast by the imposing buildings.

I remember once when I was about four years old and there was to be a party at the daycare. I'd forgotten to tell Mom that I needed to bring something for the kids that day. I knew she would be mad at my forgetfulness, but probably would not have been able to afford anything as it was. I snuck into the kitchen where my grandfather sat at the kitchen table, blind and unable to see me. He was exceptionally tall, probably around six foot three, and rawboned. He always smelled like smoke and pungent aftershave. He had the distrustful personality of all retired cops. He always knew I'd act up even before I did, except this once. I snitched some of his cigarettes out of the carton he kept in a cabinet. I thought they made a person cool. So I took the pilfered packs, and I brought them to daycare and passed them out to my friends as party favors. They didn't have a clue what they were for, but they liked any gift. I was busted when I pretended to smoke. As one would imagine, the adults were not real happy with me. They couldn't say too much when I explained to them, ever so patiently, that I was only sharing—and that sharing is caring. My mom was appalled, but my grandfather thought it was funny. For once, I'd put one over on him, and right beneath his very nose.

My cousin Taneasha thought it was the bomb. Usually she could be relied upon to kick my butt sideways just because she could, but for once, she approved. She loved to get me in trouble. I had a teddy bear that would repeat what you said to it, and she constantly egged me on to cuss at it. If I didn't cuss, she'd lock me in my bedroom until my cousin Jamie took mercy on me and let me out. He'd be mad at me for letting Taneasha get the better of me, but he always had my back.

Ours was a very large extended family; both my parents had many nearby relatives. Though they didn't help my mom overmuch when we were hurting for money, they took care of us in other ways. My dad's family was very well-to-do, thanks to lots of hard work and perseverance, and they firmly believed you had to make it on your own! It was a tough lesson to learn but also one of the most important in my life. I learned that if you really want something, you need to get it for yourself.

The Muhammad clan provided me with my first glimpses of the big, wide world and all its foibles. We travelled every year, and they taught me that understanding, compassion, and tolerance were the keys needed to face life straight on. You can't appreciate diversity if you don't truly embrace it. I was about to learn that firsthand.

As I grew older and neared kindergarten age, my mother feared what might become of me if I began my education in the area where we lived. In other words, she feared me getting a start in downtown Boston with all its troubles. Her solution was to enroll me in the METCO program. To go to kindergarten, I was bused to the suburbs, an hour's ride away. At the family daycare they hadn't taught me much of anything, so my entry into school was difficult. I was later diagnosed with ADHD (attention deficit/hyperactivity disorder), and learning would prove to be a real struggle for me. My mom tried her best to get a better life for me by sending me to school some distance from home, but it was quite an adjustment for little me. All my friends attended schools within walking distance of home; therefore, we couldn't hang out much anymore.

The suburban school I was bused to, Fisk Elementary, had a program that paired kids up with local suburban families to help them fit in. Mine was the Kieser family. Their little girl, Jennifer (whom her friends called Jenny), helped make my transition to the new school much happier!

The Kiesers were really good to me. They took me places my mom couldn't afford to take me to. When they opened their home to me on visits, I was amazed. It wasn't anything like my tiny apartment. It was a huge house with several bedrooms and many bathrooms. To me, it was palatial. They even had a maid, which I didn't understand back then, because nobody from my neighborhood had one. They'd more likely have *been* maids.

Being around the Kiesers was strange, like being in another world, because they had a traditional family with two parents and two kids. Since my dad had not been in the picture for years, I wasn't used to a family unit. I just had my mom, and she had me.

I did eventually make some friends at my new school, even though I was in the minority racially and religiously. Most of the kids were nice enough, and they were fascinated by my hair. I remember them wanting to touch it because it was strange to them and so different from theirs. Thinking about that still makes me smile.

As I continued in school, my life became more complicated. The kids there were predominately white and very rich. They had the most amazing gadgets and clothes. I didn't fit in, but it was about more than just the color of my skin. I was poor and from the proverbial wrong side of the tracks. The kids from "my" side didn't want to hang out anymore because, they said, I acted too white.

I was at Fisk Elementary School trying my best to learn and have fun, but I was stuck in limbo between two different worlds, feeling like I was living a double life. It was confusing at the time, but I felt content enough. That was all about to change drastically.

2. Innocence Taken

My parents were divorced for several years, and I was about eight when Mom met Vincent (Butch) Strother, Jr. Until then, it was just she and I, two peas in a pod, and I was happy being her second self. Butch was a state trooper, yet to me that didn't matter. Being a cop didn't make you a good guy. I didn't really like him, but I felt that as long as my mother was happy, then I was happy. It was hard moving in with him, because not only did we join him, he had two other children tagging along. I had been an only child, so you have to understand how difficult it was to share my mother with three other people. Before then, I had been the world to my mother. Mom had always been so attentive to my every need and want. Not anymore.

My mother and her sister started fighting because we had moved out of the apartment building they owned with their father (my grandfather). All of a sudden I'd lost my mom's *unconditional* approval as well as the support of my aunt. I felt lumped in with Butch, my new stepdad, and my aunt didn't like him because he was isolating my mother from her family. I feared she didn't like me anymore either, since I couldn't stop him. It all filtered down to me in my child's mind, because everything seemed to be my fault.

The move was a hard adjustment because my aunt and uncle had children who I used to be around a lot, so it felt like I was losing my sister and brothers along with my mom. Moving also meant going to a new school in Easton, Massachusetts. The town and school were very affluent, and yet once again, I was starting over and trying to fit in. This was becoming a pattern.

When I was about nine years old, my mother had a miscarriage of Butch's baby. This was hard on everyone in the family. I think Mom developed postpartum depression. She wouldn't leave the bedroom. I would try to talk with her, but she couldn't.

It was only six months later that Mom was pregnant with my sister. Despite a safe delivery this time, I don't think the depression ever lifted.

I loved my little sister, but I also resented her. Once baby sister was born, she became my only focus. This was at my parents' insistence. I was expected to care for her. Who wants to be immersed in baby formula and crappy diapers when she should be hanging out with friends, listening to music, and giggling about everything she doesn't know about sex but is too cool to admit it? I never got to hang out at the mall and experience what the other children my age were able to, like developing crushes, holding hands in a dark movie theater, and maybe stealing a first kiss. It was really hard, because I wanted to spend time with my friends from school and with my cousins. Even my stepsisters got to go away in the summer, but me, I was kept home to babysit.

Trust me, I loved my sister to death and considered her my own, but how screwed up is that? I was only ten years old! I didn't want to be a mom or even a wife, for that matter, but Butch had other, more sinister plans for me. It just took a while for them to be realized.

We moved around a lot over the next two years. I remember living in Taunton, Canton, and Berkley. When I was around twelve years old, we were living in Taunton. It is a small town situated some forty miles south of Boston. It had a population of about fifty-five thousand spread out over forty-eight square miles and is recognized as one of the oldest towns in America. It was established in 1637 by members of the original Plymouth

Colony. Taunton was beautiful and serene, with historic houses and mills clustered on tree-lined streets. It seemed like a great place to move to...at first.

I started middle school. That's when I discovered that I liked girls. As if my life were not confusing enough, I suspected I was gay. God had to be sitting in heaven laughing his omniscient head off! Didn't I have enough on my plate raising and taking care of my siblings and being forced to play housewife, plus doing all the chores? I had to be a freak, too?

I made the colossal mistake of telling my mom about a dream I'd had one night where I was kissing a girl and liked it. We'd not had a healthy enough relationship since my stepfather had come into the picture for her to handle this very well. So, of course, she broke my confidence and told Butch all about it. To a man who had already enslaved a preadolescent girl, this was a taunt and a direct challenge to his manhood. He couldn't let that slide, could he? Well, believe me, he sure didn't. He now had a reason to perform his sinister intentions.

I was finally introduced to my stepfather, for real. I'd never actually looked at him as a man, so much as just the guy my mom had married. He was not very attractive on the outside. He was overweight, was missing several teeth, and had a fake eye. He used to gross me out, especially when that eye would fall out and he would make me go look for it.

We were sitting in a scruffy secondhand minivan, alone, when I saw him as he truly was: a black-hearted, evil devil. He decided to teach me a lesson, and I want to puke every time I recall it. He ruined my first kiss. He grabbed me and kissed me. It was not some innocent peck with another kid, but full tongue over bare, slimy gums. Ugh! I was completely freaked out, and much worse, I was absolutely terrified of what he was doing to me. I was just a baby. What was he thinking? I know what I was thinking right then: *Is this just a bad dream, or is it something else?* He was the only father figure I had. My biological father wasn't in the picture much anymore, because Butch didn't want him around at all. I never prayed so hard in my life that my lesson had been well learned and that being kissed by a man was all I needed to

9

be taught. I was hoping he would never try it again. I was hoping it would stop there. I was petrified.

All of a sudden, taking care of the kids and the house wasn't so bad. Just please, God, let me not have to start taking care of him! Please!

Even today, twenty years later, I can recall every second of my next lesson. I break into a sweat and shudder at the shame I still feel. Dammit, I was only twelve years old, and completely innocent!

That evening I'd put all the kids to bed and had fallen asleep on the floor in front of the TV in my mom's room. I was rewinding *Beauty and the Beast*, which my siblings watched before bed every night. I remember the ugly rug and the flickering TV, and the terror I felt when I awoke with lips on mine! Butch was kissing me again! Oh man, even today, more than twenty years later, if I smell Old Spice aftershave I gag, and breathing becomes difficult because the panic still haunts me.

Butch was kissing me with that gross mouth and leering at me with those screwed-up, mismatched eyes. There was none of God's laughter in my head then. Instead of laughter, there was revulsion. How could this be happening? Where was my mother? Who was protecting me? Then he was touching me where no one had touched me before.

He began massaging my immature breasts, his excited sickness making him pant. I was panicking! It was awful, and then it got worse. He reached down between my legs and began groping me. I was frozen with fear and shame. I'd never even been on a date, besides which, I was too young and way too busy raising his kids. This wasn't fair. What's going on? Why me, little Kathryn?

I remember Butch pulling off my shirt and yanking down my pants as he explained he was only teaching me something. My lesson was to be my first orgasm, which he guaranteed would be the last of its kind that I would ever experience.

I was scared and tense. He laid me down and told me to be quiet before he lowered his filthy mouth and proceeded to go down on me. He ate me until I had an orgasm. After he finished, he told me again that this would be the first and last time I would ever experience orgasm like that. I didn't understand what he meant. I was so ashamed of the way it had felt. I wasn't supposed to feel like that with him. As innocent as I was, I instinctively at least knew that much: this was wrong, and I must have done something really bad to have asked for it. I just didn't know what I could possibly have done to bring this upon myself. Butch left me lying there wreathed in guilt and then went about his business, disappearing somewhere in the house. I clambered up off the floor and stumbled to the bathroom to scrub off his lingering presence. No amount of scrubbing could accomplish that. It didn't work. I was stuck with his sickening touch forever.

What was I supposed to do now? I was scared, and I didn't think I should (or even could) tell Mom or call the police. Butch was a state trooper, after all, who was supposed to serve and protect. I didn't think anyone would believe me. I just thought and hoped and prayed in my little girl way that it wouldn't happen again.

Afterward, I was terribly confused and wracked with guilt. How could something so wrong feel so good? I decided that I wasn't going to ever let it feel good again. That's what I promised to myself!

To this day, his words that I would never be able to orgasm like that again still stick in my head. Whenever I have made love to someone through the years, I have constantly had to have a conversation in my mind to tell myself it is OK. I have to reassure myself that it's not my stepfather touching me. If I don't or can't talk to myself, then I seek escape by taking myself out of my body. I taught myself this coping mechanism. It's my protection. Leaving my body and looking away enabled me to handle the abuse through those difficult years.

Some may wonder why I didn't seek help sooner, or why I let it go on for such a long time. They forget that I was but a child. Please tell me, where in the world does a twelve-year-old go? I wanted to escape and run away. The main reason I stayed at home was that I was raising my younger siblings. I loved them so very much and wanted to protect them. My mother no longer worked, so I knew that she wouldn't have the income to support them were we all to run away from Butch. I also knew that once I breathed a word about what was really happening in our house, things would never be the same. Telling would be a point of no return and I knew that once it got out, there would be no way to turn things back. Back then I was really close to my siblings. We now had a baby brother in the family. I felt as though Mom's and Butch's children were all my children. I was terrified of the changes that would result if I spoke up and dared to tell anyone about what was going on, about what was happening to me, and what I was hiding in my aching heart.

Butch's attentions continued and became much worse through the next four years. Here's something he made me do regularly. Every day I had to bring him his gun, but on the days when he would start up our sessions, things would become much more sinister. The pistol I had to bring him wasn't always his service revolver. Sometimes it was an old gun that he kept on top of the refrigerator in a crystal bowl. Every time I brought him either weapon, I felt it was a silent warning of the consequences should I not submit to his wishes. I had moved beyond terror to abject acceptance of my situation. Nobody would ever help me now.

I would obey him, but he soon learned that I was stubborn and wouldn't orgasm no matter how long he stayed down on me, gun or no gun. Sometimes he'd try for what seemed like hours and my poor crotch would be raw from his whiskers. Even if my body betrayed me he never knew. I would not give him the satisfaction. He'd ruined his own plaything.

Before our house in Berkley was built, we had to live in a hotel for several months. My mother, stepfather, two stepsisters, baby sister, baby brother, and I all shared one room. It was all wet towels, dirty laundry, baby poop, and no solitude. It sucked! My stepsisters and I would all sleep on the floor at night. I really don't know how I passed school that year, because it was really hard to get any peace or quiet in the room when I had homework.

They say that every cloud has a silver lining. That terrible, cramped little hotel room became heaven and a haven for me!

There was nowhere for Butch to drag me off to for any "special" time together. I got a break, and for a while I was almost happy.

When the new house was finished and we were moving in, everyone was so excited—except for me. How could I be? It had so many rooms, on two levels, and unlike in the hotel room, I could no longer hide from my stepdad in plain sight.

Up until then, things had stopped at oral sex, but since I wouldn't orgasm that way anymore, Butch decided a new lesson was in order. Back then, I used to sleep anywhere in the house where there were siblings and never alone in my room. That way I could protect myself. For the first time in my life, I had my own bedroom. But I was afraid to sleep in it!

My final lesson began in the middle of the night. I think it must have been around two o'clock. Some of the memories are vivid. I can remember waking up in Butch's arms as he carried me downstairs, away from my sleeping family. What I don't remember is why he took me to my stepsisters' room instead of to mine. I couldn't really inquire at the time, but looking back, maybe he was demonstrating that he alone held the power. He was in control and could do whatever he wanted, wherever he wanted, and heaven help anyone trying to stop him!

I woke up as he carried me down the stairs. That awful scent of Old Spice invaded my nose. I wanted to scream for help, to struggle and run away—anything but travel downward and into my next nightmare. I knew it was useless to protest. I nearly went insane when it came to me that he was carrying a jar of Vaseline. We never used that before! What did he need Vaseline for?

He turned left at the bottom of the stairs and carried me to one of the twin beds there in the room. He put me down on the bed and stripped off my pajamas while I cried inside. I never cried tears on the outside anymore. As hard as it was, there was no way I would give him the satisfaction of knowing how deeply I was suffering.

I did not want to be naked in this room on this bed with him hovering over me like some avaricious, territorial lion. I didn't want him going down on me because I knew one day he'd just eat me alive and that'd be the end of me. As it turned out, I would much rather he'd have done that instead.

For years, Butch's routine varied little. He'd strip me down mentally with his gun and physically with his hands. Then he'd have his way with me with his mouth. That night was different, completely different.

I heard that unmistakable sound when he opened the Vaseline jar followed by an unknown, prolonged rhythmic noise after he'd removed his pants. It was dark in the room, even though the windows weren't covered up by drapes or blinds. There must not have been any moonlight that night. It was pitch black outside, just like the darkness of this secret life of mine: no light and no color.

He climbed on top of me, not like he'd ever done before. Immediately he went for full penetration, scaring me to death. I reacted instantly and clamped down so tight that he couldn't get his erect penis all the way into me. It hurt so bad that I felt that my private place between my legs, which he had abused with his mouth for so many years, had been ripped wide open. I wanted to pass out and I wanted to scream bloody murder and I wanted my mommy. He could tell I was ready to lose it and growled in my ear warning me to be quiet, or else. It pissed him off that he couldn't get all the way inside me, no matter how hard it was or how hard he tried. Besides my being tiny in frame, my insides were tiny too. I was only a little fourteen-year-old. He'd truly stolen the rest of my innocence now, innocence in every sense of the word. The rape of the body, mind, and spirit of me, Kathryn Harriet Muhammad, was complete.

Eventually, the torture of his pounding body came to an end and I thought it was over. He pushed up off of my body and yanked his penis from my tender insides. The excruciating pain was so intense that I would have cried out, except that his ugly face was right in mine, and he told me I needed to learn to loosen up.

What he didn't know was that he'd trained me to clamp down during the years of oral sex. I'd crush any tingling sensation that might lead to an orgasm by flexing my vaginal muscles together. Like I said, he'd ruined his own sex toy.

As he was leaving the room, one-eyed Butch turned to me and told me we'd have more fun, but that what I needed to do was to not be so tense. That way he could enjoy it more. The bastard!

When the pain subsided enough so that I could get up and walk, I crawled off the bed and managed to stagger to my room. I was completely overcome by the agony of what he'd done and the anguish in my soul. I couldn't take much more from him. I wanted to die that night, but since that wasn't about to happen and since I had somehow survived, what I needed and wanted was a shower to clean myself out and get rid of his stench. We were forbidden to take too many showers, and the sound of the flowing water might have awakened my mom, but I had one anyway. What would I have said if she had come downstairs that night? Would I have told her then? I wish she had come down and caught me. I wish with my whole being that she would have supported me and taken my side against her husband, my tormentor. I lay in my bed throbbing with pain, envisioning my mom rescuing me from the hell I was in.

The alarm for school came very soon after I had finally fallen into a fitful sleep. I was too tired and bruised to go to school, yet I knew that I would find some comfort there from the structure and the presence of others around me. I almost felt safe there, even though I was living a huge lie, walking around acting like everything in my world was mighty fine.

After all that's gone on since that night, I wonder how I survived. I was traumatized at fourteen years old by a more intense form of abuse than what he'd been doing to me for years. It had such a profound effect on my psyche that even today, so many years later, I still clamp down and fight automatically against any pleasure. I literally have to tell myself now that it is OK to feel good when I'm being touched. That it is OK to be scared and to work through it. It is OK to be mad about what happened. And more important, it is OK to cry for myself and the little girl whose innocence was taken by force. None of it was my fault!

I made it through school the day after that horrible night when Butch raped me the first time, and I wonder how it could be that nobody noticed the difference in me. I guess I had learned to hide my feelings quite well, thanks to all the practice I'd had since I was twelve. I felt significant changes emerging in me from that very day on. I had always been a good girl, even when my cousin Taneasha was bribing and threatening me to cuss at my teddy bear and I wouldn't do it, but now, all of a sudden, I wanted to fight back wherever I could. I couldn't worry so much about what everyone thought of me, and I needed to toughen up. Cursing no longer seemed to be a cardinal sin, so I decided I'd cuss right along with all the other kids.

I'm sure it doesn't seem like that was very much, but I felt a little more in control once I had come to the decision to break free a bit and make my own decisions about some things. I guess that I needed to feel some kind of empowerment. That new strength lasted about as long as it took for it to dawn on me that now I had really had sex and that that was how a girl gets pregnant. Talk about a cold shower all over the warmth of my budding strength.

I had been a decent student until then. Sure, it was difficult for me to learn because of the ADHD, but I worked hard at it. I was the student council president at the time, and it had helped a lot for me to feel important and powerful in that position instead of what I was at home: the maid, housewife, babysitter, and reluctant sex toy. Imagine the terror I felt, knowing that my perceived position, importance, and power would mean nothing if Butch had made me pregnant. When it crossed my mind that I could be pregnant, I froze inside, because no achievements would matter if I was expecting a baby, especially a baby by my mother's husband.

When those thoughts hit me, I was electrified by fear. I jumped up in class and asked for a bathroom pass. When I got there, I locked myself in a stall and began pounding on my stomach, crying and nearly hysterical, screaming in my head over and over that there cannot be a baby, that there must not be a baby. I kept punching myself in that stinky little stall until I was exhausted and overwhelmed by terror as I kept thinking of what might happen. Maybe Butch would kill me if it became known I was carrying his baby. It didn't dawn on me that if I was going to be a mother, it would be entirely Butch's fault. Why would I not be the one to blame? Everything that had happened to me already had to be my fault, right? Why would this be any different?

Through the next few months, I struggled through my classes at Somerset High School. My stepsisters had many personal issues there, so our parents pulled us out of it and moved us to Bristol Plymouth Technical School. To me, thinking back, it seems ridiculous that they never noticed that I might be battling huge personal demons myself. They probably wouldn't have cared if they had!

The move to a different school turned out to be a new start for me, but at the same time, it marked the beginning of the end of my life as I knew it. The abuse continued through the remainder of that year and during most of the next. By that time, I was a freshman in high school.

I made a new friend at Bristol Plymouth Technical, and for the first time in my life, I felt that I could trust someone. We didn't get to see each other outside of school, because I wasn't allowed to visit and stuff, and besides, I wouldn't have had time anyway. Still, I was delighted, even though for just a brief period, to have a friend who could maybe share my burden and help save me from myself.

I had contemplated suicide for so many years that I knew if I didn't come clean at this point, I was going to kill myself. My stepfather still made me bring his loaded gun to him before our time together. One day I was walking up the stairs taking the revolver to him when I knew I'd had enough. I put the gun in my mouth. I was about to pull the trigger when my little sister came home and called for me. I had tears in my eyes as I gagged on the metallic taste of the gun barrel. I couldn't do this to her. She was right by the staircase, and Thomasina would have been the first one to find me splattered all over the walls. She saved my life that day. If it wasn't for her running and calling for me, that would have been the end. Nobody but Butch would have known why I was so emotionally and physically drained, or how much sorrow and pain I'd suffered at his hands.

Since I had decided that my friend and I had become really close, the next day at school and following a major psychological battle with myself about what I should do, I sucked it all up, decided I could trust her, and told her what was happening. I had kept this secret for so long without being able to talk to anyone about the sexual abuse that I thought I was going to hyperventilate and then die before I'd ever get anything out. I couldn't catch my breath and I didn't die, but I did admit it, finally.

God, what a colossal step I'd taken. I was petrified and sweaty and relieved all in the same moment. After the shock of what I'd done wore off, it felt good to have confided in someone. It was an enormous relief to talk about it. I had felt so alone for years. My school friend supported me and commiserated about my situation, trying to empathize. I can imagine it was hard for somebody who wasn't even old enough to drive to understand the depth of trust and desperation it required of me to open up to her, but she tried her very best. Responding to my pain, she pushed me to tell an adult. I shut down completely on that idea.

My friend, immaturity notwithstanding, was smart enough to know she couldn't responsibly keep this secret to herself. With a bitten conscience, she told a guidance counselor about what was happening with her best friend. I wasn't too scared when I was called down to the office, because I had told the girl not to say anything to anyone about the abuse. I guess she knew I really needed the help. Nevertheless, when I was going through the pain and humiliation of being queried by the counselor and at the same time not wanting to get myself into trouble, I was furious with her.

The counselor asked me to talk about it with her. She told me I wouldn't get into trouble and that I could trust her. I so wanted to break the silence. I wanted to be free and get over all the pain and worry that I had been living with for so long. I knew it wasn't that simple. She said, "Your friend told me you are being abused." My mouth just dropped open as I thought that I had to think up something real fast. So I prevaricated and told her it wasn't about me, but about a friend of mine at another school, and that I had promised not to tell anyone. She tried for a long time to get me to talk. I wouldn't, because I was so frightened of the consequences that revealing my secret to the authorities would bring.

I was terrified that the counselor was going to call my parents and that my mom would finally know and have to choose either him or me. I was eventually sent back to class. It felt like a trip to the gallows. I was shaking inside and my stomach was queasy. My teacher was seriously concerned by my demeanor when I returned to my classroom and sent me to see the nurse. It blows my mind to think that those three people, the counselor, my teacher, and the nurse, who were there to take care of me, never talked to one another about me. If they had, they could have connected the dots, and my future could very well have been much different.

The guidance counselor didn't call my parents, but she hadn't forgotten about me. A week later, she called me to her office again and asked me to tell her the truth. I kept to my lie and said it was someone from another school and that it wasn't me who was being abused. She told me that if I ever wanted to talk, the door would always be open.

I never told her or spoke to her after that, and I never spoke to my friend again. My secret was out, and I walked around in a numbed daze waiting for the other shoe to drop. I was so tense and panicky that I couldn't concentrate. Why didn't anybody at school notice? I was flipping out, and nobody cared there in the one place where I had always felt somewhat safe and protected. I was totally alone now. My isolation was complete.

After about a month, as the new personal hell I was living in dragged on, I noticed my stepfather starting to act really weird. He was in some kind of legal trouble, but I didn't know what it was about and I didn't want to ask Mom. They didn't tell me anything, because they thought I was too young. What a load of crap! Here they'd forced me into adulthood at the age of ten, and my stepfather had forced me into womanhood by age twelve! What did they think I couldn't handle? I'd laugh, except it wasn't very funny at all!

Around Christmas, my stepsister told my stepfather that I had said something to her about the way he was acting and that

I had asked her if she knew what was going on. I would never have said anything to him myself, because I was so scared of him. After she told him of my curiosity, Butch got in my face and bellowed at me that he never loved or wanted me and that it was none of my fucking business. He demanded to know what made me think he wanted me when he didn't want any children. Yes, I was being abused by him, but since he was the only father I had for so many years, his words really hurt. I remember tearing helter-skelter downstairs to my room and just crying hysterically. That was a total waste of emotion. What did I really think—that he had been raping me all these years because he loved me?

Afterward, I was scared to go back upstairs, and I was sure at this point that either he was going to kill me or that I was going to commit suicide. I couldn't take the stress any longer, and I needed to either leave or die. I had stayed around long enough to see my siblings grow up a little bit, as I had raised them and had dearly loved and nurtured them. Now I faced a dilemma: to somehow manage to save myself or to end my life.

Later, when I had calmed down some, I turned on the television, and it was really weird when a teen help line advertisement came on. It was about some new national campaign to help teens in need. I had never seen anything like this before. It intrigued me and I wanted to call right away, but I didn't. Maybe I couldn't bring myself to do it right then, but I did write down the number and hid it under my socks in the dresser drawer. Life moved on.

My school friend had noticed I was in a bad way, and even though I wouldn't talk to her anymore, she really wanted to help—or at least that's what I guessed at the time. So then what happened? She told my stepsister what was happening to me at home. My stepsister asked me if this was true. I answered truthfully and said yes. I told her not to dare say anything to anyone. Of course, that didn't work. She kept telling me to tell our mom, but I was determined not to. Now I was scared to say anything to anyone. The cat was now out of the bag.

The night my stepsister told my mother, Mom hollered for me to come see her and asked me point blank if the story was true. I asked stupidly, "If what was true?" She said I knew what she was talking about. I stood there panicking and didn't say a single, solitary word. Here was the moment I had been waiting for. I had suffered for four years at Butch's hands, and the time had finally come when Mom would help me. Yet I was speechless.

I gripped my trembling hands behind my back and just held them there. I looked around my mom's room and wondered how such an everyday place had become such a torture chamber. The bed was the same as always with its flowery bedspread, nothing scary there, and the walls were still white with no dripping blood or gore. The window blinds hadn't turned to snakes and no monster jumped out of the closet, but I was in complete and utter agony. I felt that my entire body was engulfed in flames—a searing agony of heat, ignited by my shame. What was I supposed to say?

She roared at me that she wanted an answer. At that moment, a powerful calm descended on me and finally, after what seemed like hours, I stared her straight in the eyes and told her yes, and then yes again, that it was true. My heart stopped at the look on her face. It was a face I had never seen before, and I didn't know what that look meant.

My mom, beside herself with upset, then marched downstairs and forced me to go with her. I didn't want to accompany her, because I knew she was extremely angry. I wasn't sure if her anger was centered on Butch or on me. I don't know how I made it down the steps. My legs were so wobbly, and I definitely felt faint.

She accosted Butch and blurted it out to him. She wanted to know if it was true that he had been sleeping with me. He was so shocked that my mother instantly knew that I was telling the truth. I think it really caught him off guard, because he just said a simple yes. Could it be that maybe he wanted her to know? He calmly pointed out that he was only trying to teach me something. There was a dead silence. I was elated that the truth was out! I couldn't believe Butch had admitted it to Mother. I thought that now she would take me in her arms and rock me and shelter me from her husband, the monster in our midst. I thought that she'd love me again like she had before he came around and they got married.

Nothing happened! My mother told me to go upstairs and get the kids ready for bed as if a grenade hadn't just been dropped in the middle of the room. My vilest living nightmare had been exposed, and my mom was worried about the kids' stupid teeth being brushed! What was she thinking about? She obviously wasn't thinking about me! This was not how this tragedy's end was supposed to unfold! Dammit!

My mother came back upstairs alone and told me that she was going for a ride with my stepfather and that she would be back. I was absolutely stunned. I was both furious and terrified, and yet I still wouldn't cry. Why wasn't she murdering him or kicking him out? Why didn't she hold me and tell me it wasn't my fault?

I was emotionally wrung out as I tucked my younger siblings into bed. I just wanted to hold them to me and let their innocence embrace me like it had from the time they were born. From the time I was ten, I was forever adorned by a child on my hip. Much of my childhood was spent toting two babies, one on each hip, and as tiny as I was, people were amazed that I could hold onto and manage them both. Often when I put them to bed, I'd cradle them on my chest and I'd pretend I was keeping them safe, while all along it was their tiny warm bodies, with their beating hearts and baby breath, that were comforting me and sheltering me from my tortured soul.

That night I knew without a doubt that my innocence was lost forever and life would never be the same. I knew something was horribly wrong. I stood amidst the children's beds, staring at them. I wanted to stay and protect them and knew I couldn't. The kind of love I'd always wanted from my mother and hadn't had since I was a baby poured forth from me to engulf them. I finally cried then, after a four-year drought of tears, for the happy baby I'd once been and for the abused shell of a little girl I'd become and, yes, I cried for fear of what the future would hold.

When those anguished tears dried, I swore I would never show that much emotion again. I would never let anyone know how crushed I was by the loss of my childhood innocence. A stoic face would be shown to my mother whenever she finally got back. Childish tears would have no place in my future. I wasn't a child any longer, after all.

Later, all of my siblings and I were in my mom's room trying to get some sleep. My parents had been gone for hours, and when I heard the bedroom door open, I pretended I was sleeping. I didn't want to talk about any of this awful business with her. I was in a psychological and emotional void, quite unable to understand why she'd left me at such a pivotal moment in my life. My mother shook me awake and told me to follow her downstairs. I shuffled along behind her as if in a fog.

There he sat in my bedroom, where he had put his computer on a stand by my closet. It wasn't bad enough that he had invaded my body; he'd even invaded my space. Not that it mattered, because to me, my bedroom was a white-and-brown prison cell where I had no cherished personal belongings; they were just sleeping quarters. He was typing away when we walked in like it was business as usual or something, and nothing more than that.

My stepfather turned to me and casually apologized and told me he shouldn't have done what he did to me. I looked at him like he was crazy, because it was like he was apologizing for stepping on my toe or something. I barely heard him as he promised not to do it again since I had learned my lesson. Maybe worse, and unfortunately for me, the only thing my mother could focus on was who I had told. I stated that I'd only told a friend. She then insisted that I had to lie and say it never happened.

I was like: *What the fuck?*

Butch, my stepfather and my mother's husband, admits to forcing me to have sex with him, and my mother tells me that I have to tell everyone that I, the offended party, had lied and that Butch had never tried anything with me. At that moment I lost all respect for my mother. I hated her. I couldn't believe that she could ask me to do something like this. Why was this happening to me? What did I do wrong? My knees buckled and I fell back onto the bed. Butch then calmly said that if I didn't say I lied and that if he lost his other kids because of me, then he would kill me. I didn't need to look at him to know that this threat was deadly serious. I just cried inside myself: furious, invisible tears that I refused to reveal to them, my tormentors, my supposed protectors, my parents. My stepfather had abused me sexually for four years, and now he and Mother threaten me and order me to lie about it, just when the truth had been exposed. I sat there in a daze as she told me that in the morning I must tell my stepsisters that I had lied about the sexual abuse.

Beginning the next day and from the very moment I lied about the abuse to my siblings; I no longer had a close relationship with them. They no longer trusted me, because I'd said horrible things about their dad. We haven't really spoken since. It was devastating, because everyone I cared about seemed to be slipping through my fingers, myself included.

The morning when I lied to my stepsisters was the same morning that my mother took me to the grocery store and bought herself a pack of cigarettes. She hadn't smoked in over six years. She said it would calm her nerves. I thought she ought to give me one too, since I was traveling through hell on earth. What, did she think that I wasn't feeling anything? As the Newport's smoke streamed out of her mouth and billowed around the inside of the car, she told me I had to go to school and tell my friend I had lied. I was mesmerized by the smoke puffing out with her every word. Each puff could have been a nail in my coffin, because she was killing me. Wasn't it painful enough that she had forced me to tell my stepsisters that I lied? Now my friend had to be told, too? I hadn't been speaking to her anyway, because of her betrayal to the school counselor. My friend would think I was insane. Despite my conscience, Mother was still the boss, and I'd do what she said because I wasn't strong enough to go against her quite yet.

When I got home that afternoon, I told her it was done. She got up from the kitchen table where she'd been chain smoking and threw the cigarettes into the trash. She said she wouldn't need them anymore, because there was nothing to worry about now. I stared at those cigarettes in the trash. How symbolic was that? It was as if she'd thrown me in there with them, just a lying piece of garbage. She broke my heart, and worse, she broke my spirit.

School was agony after that for me. The place where I had always felt fairly safe was now ruined for me. I was spooked and felt everyone knew and was looking at me and laughing. I became so numb. I was angry at the world, and I didn't care to even be in it anymore. I kept asking God, *Why me?* I floated around in a haze the remainder of the time I spent there, because nothing really mattered now. I didn't think there was one human being in the building, or the world, who could relate to my situation or empathize with me.

One especially bad day, when I got home I watched television again, and the same commercial for teens in need, abused kids, and runaways came on the screen. I had forgotten the number tucked into my sock drawer. I decided to call. I needed someone to save me, or at least to hear me. My mother wasn't protecting me; she hadn't since I was a baby. I needed help. They said it was anonymous and that they wouldn't call anyone unless you were ready.

So I dialed the number and I talked to a guy. He asked me politely the reason for the call. He was really soft spoken and told me it was OK to talk to him. There was a searing tension in my chest as I debated what to tell him. I could not handle the idea of anyone else judging me, even though he was a stranger. He was very cool and calm and without rushing or pressuring me, he conveyed the feeling that he really cared and that it was better to talk about it. What a relief! I told him everything that was going on. It all came pouring out in a torrent of words and feelings, and as I reached the heartrending part about having to lie, I was sobbing. He listened, didn't judge, and maybe saved my life. We talked for quite a while.

Eventually, he told me that I needed to call the police or talk with my guidance counselor. He said he could make the calls if I wanted him to. I mentioned to him that Christmas was coming up soon and I didn't want to ruin it for my siblings. There was a pregnant pause as he digested that comment. I think he was amazed that I could think of anyone but myself at a time like this, and he asked who was worrying about *me*. Yeah, what about me? Nobody I was supposed to matter to seemed to give a crap.

He pushed a little bit more about calling someone, and I became afraid that maybe the conversation was being recorded or traced. I just hung up on him.

Not long after Christmas, I reached a point where I'd had enough of everything, of everyone acting like it hadn't happened and that I was a pariah for saying it had. If I didn't leave now, I was going to kill myself one way or another, but probably with Butch's gun. I told myself that whatever I had to do, I would. Even if I had to live on the streets, that's what I was going to do. I'd persevere because I wanted to live, just to prove I could.

The guy on the help line I called before Christmas? He saved my life. Even though I'd hung up on him and didn't really let him help me, I had, through his compassionate voice, unearthed the slender ray of hope that since he believed me and was willing to help me, Kathryn, maybe there was someone else who would also be willing to help me. I grasped onto this as an article of faith, that somebody might help who wasn't a stranger to me. I held on for dear life.

3. The Struggle to Survive

Looking back, I can still remember the night I left home as if it were yesterday. I get a little giddy reflecting on how I'd finally worked up the nerve to run and that outside of what I wore out the door, I had absolutely no plans. What a dork I was. I didn't think it through at all. I just got dressed and left. But I'm also so very proud of me, of that fifteen-year-old little girl I was. She took her life in her hands, knew she'd had enough, and dragged herself up out of hell and into an unknown future. I had survived being a preemie, the divorce of my parents, raising all my siblings, years of sexual abuse, and being thrown into the trash. I was determined to endure and to fight back at whatever might come my way.

I didn't know what I was thinking. All I knew with certainty was that I was getting out and that I was not coming back. I didn't care that it was a freezing Massachusetts night. All I put on was a running suit. I figured that if I got spotted by the police, a running outfit wouldn't draw attention to me. It was about two in the morning when I left home with no money, no food, and no jacket.

I stepped through the door of the house that everyone but me had been so thrilled to move into. I closed the door behind me and reached out to make sure I had locked it. I didn't have or need a key, because I was never coming back. That thought gave me pause as I looked up at the front of the building that I had never felt was my home. It looked exactly the same as it had every day when I came home from school, with its bricks and mortar and windows, but this time I didn't plan to ever see it again. It looked pretty and serene with the moonlight twinkling off of the window panes. That house would appear to be a safe haven to anybody, but not to me, because for me it had been a torturous prison. I turned my back on it for good and trotted down the steps.

The night air was truly frosty as I scuttled to the safety of the street. It froze my nose hairs and caught at my breath. My eyes were on fire. They wanted to water, but it was just too cold. As I sped into my unknown future, the condensation from my freezing breath swirled up and disappeared into the night like tiny ghosts escaping their own eternal interment. I felt like some of the fear, angst, and hate floated away from me, into the darkness, with my breath.

I walked in the frigid gloom, shrouded by the skeletal, barren trees along the roadside, for about an hour. I was heading north toward Taunton, alone but not afraid, when a cop pulled over and asked what I was doing. I had planned my lie and said I was just out training for track, not even knowing that track is run in springtime, not in the dead of winter.

He put me in the back of the patrol car, climbed back into the front, laid his arm across the back of the seat, and swiveled around to look at me. I avoided eye contact. I gazed at the frosted windows with their ice patterns that looked like snowflakes. I felt like I was in an ice castle. It calmed me down.

He asked if I was a runaway, and I denied it. I remember him being young and white. He stared at me while his fingers drummed the passenger headrest. He was chomping on gum with a loud, smacking noise. I wanted to laugh, thinking that my grandma would've let him have it for chewing with his mouth open, but it wasn't the time or place for levity. He drove to a shelter not far from my house and asked the counselor if I was one of theirs. When they denied me, he asked for my address. As he drove me there, I broke into a sweat and was cussing up a storm in my head. I was thinking, *Do you know how fucking long it took me to get where I am right now, to decide to finally freaking leave? And this jerk of a cop is delivering me back to my personal hell.* I was fuming. *Shit! What if he wakes my folks?* I was doomed.

He lectured me about how it was dangerous to be out so late. It was laughable, really, with him not knowing how much more dangerous it was for me inside that lovely, despicable house. Thankfully, he was either a lazy turd or too comfy in his warm car. He just let me out and watched as I mounted the steps. Then he sped off.

After the warmth of the police car, I was twice as cold as before. I skipped down the stairs, happy I hadn't lost my freedom, and ran for real until I was winded.

That time, I made it to Taunton, which was about four miles from my house. It was necessary to lie down for a little bit to recoup my strength. The emotional impact of what I'd done was overwhelming me. I was exhausted from my escape efforts, freezing because it's brutally cold in New England in winter, and I was so hungry. I couldn't remember the last time I'd eaten. I found the place where I had lived years earlier. I'd known this area quite well from taking my siblings on walks in their strollers. I expected that if I fell asleep anywhere, this would be the safest place to be. After about an hour of not getting a wink of sleep on the ground underneath the umbrella of a pine tree, I was done roughing it. I sat up and took an appreciative sniff of the tree's fragrance. It reminded me of the sad, little Christmas tree still sitting in the living room at home—well, what I used to call home. I heaved a sigh of regret and registered that the ground beneath was freezing me. I was scared to hang around outside in the predawn haze where someone might see me and send for the cops to take me home.

When I emerged from under that tree, all my extremities tingled. I smacked my hands awake, stomped my frozen feet, and teetered on numbed legs through the sleepy town to Dunkin Donuts. My nostrils felt as though they were frozen shut when

I finally got there, and I took a great big sniff as I walked in. I didn't have any money, so I couldn't eat. The girl asked me if I wanted anything, but I told her that I was all right; I was just warming up for a second after my jog. I hid from direct sight and took a nap. I knew I couldn't stay there too long, though. I was afraid they would call the cops.

They didn't have a pay phone, so I knew I needed to get to someplace with a phone to call for help. I walked to Walmart. I knew from going shopping there with my mother that they had a phone I could use. I was scared to ask someone for change to call an old friend, but I needed to. I tried calling for about an hour, remembering after the first call to hang up before the answering machine came on. I couldn't spend the morning asking for change; Walmart would boot me out for panhandling. There was no answer at my old friend's house. Her family just wasn't home.

I remembered where she lived from being on the bus riding to and from school. I tried retracing the bus route. I found her house, but she wasn't there. I stayed there for a long time before the neighbor asked me if I needed anything. I told her I was looking for my friend but she wasn't home. She asked me if I needed to call someone. I told her yes. She invited me into her house. The only person I thought to call was my cousin Taneasha. I prayed she still had the same number from years ago, the last time we spoke.

It's odd who you think of to call for help when you are in a jam, isn't it? Taneasha was about three years older than I was. I'd spent my happier days as a child living in one of three apartments in a building my grandfather owned. Taneasha and Jamie lived in one of the other units. As a kid, she'd been a bundle of attitude and sass. She had an opinion about everything and generally required you to share it, or else. She'd stand with a hand on her cocked hip, her big, dark chocolate eyes shooting sparks, her full lips pursed, and she'd give you this stare that dared you to dispute her authority. She was the one who would kick my butt sideways just because she could, and the one who'd lock me in the bedroom if I wouldn't cuss at my teddy bear. She would bully me in a very sisterly fashion. I think her sheer orneriness as

30

a kid is what made me call her. Maybe she'd use it to my benefit for once.

Thankfully, when I called her she answered right away. I hadn't spoken to her in years because of the feud between my mom and her mom, my aunt, and for this reason, she knew something must have been wrong. She asked me what it was, and I told her I had run away from home. There was no judgment in her voice, and I almost cried when she asked me where I was so she could come get me. I told her I didn't know where I was exactly, just at a friend's house. Taneasha told me to walk to a gas station so that she would be able to find me. I ventured back into the cold, sunny day, and my cheeks and lungs had to freeze before I realized I had succumbed to tears. Great, gusting sobs broke from me at the thought that I might have a friend to turn to who wasn't a stranger. I gave myself a minute of relief before making myself stop crying. There were to be no more tears.

She must've made that twenty-three mile drive from Randolph to Taunton in record time, because it was less than an hour after cruising gas stations, looking for the street I was on, that she was able to find me. Boy, was I happy to see her. I knew she would protect me. I could trust my cousin Taneasha.

At this point, she didn't even know why I had run away from home. She just hugged and kissed me and told me everything would be OK, and then whisked me to her home. We chatted about inconsequential topics on the way back to Randolph. After we arrived, she told me to just relax as she tucked me into her bed. She wanted me to sleep, because she knew I'd been up all night and that whatever was the matter was very consequential, and I would need a clear head to tell it to her. I drifted off dreaming that she and I could be like sisters again, albeit combative ones, like we'd been before Butch had come around. Anything would be better than where I'd been with my family.

When I finally woke up, I was starving and thirsty. I had walked for about four hours in the early hours of the night without any food or water, but something to eat and drink would have to wait a little longer. Taneasha knew something huge had happened to make someone as mild mannered as I was bolt from home. We huddled on her bed and I fumbled around, sketching out the details as I told her about the nightmare of a life I had been living for so long. It took me forever. How do you tell such intimate things to someone who, despite being a cousin, is in reality a veritable stranger? We hadn't really spent time together since I had been about six or seven years old, and this wasn't kid stuff.

I didn't know if she would believe me, but if she did, would she tell me to hide from the truth as my parents had? I was extremely emotional, since my mother had told me to lie and never to tell anyone else what had happened. Taneasha disregarded that stupid piece of advice from my mother and patiently dragged the sad tale out of me. She told me her family had never particularly liked Butch because of his controlling nature. My dear cousin was devastated to learn that he'd taken his control to such an extreme, sadistic level with me. Taneasha told me not to worry, and when I refused to let her tell my aunt, she promised to keep my secret. She told me she wouldn't let anyone hurt me anymore. Those were the sweetest words I'd ever heard.

She told me that I could live with her and her mom, my Aunt Estelle, who said I could stay with them with one provision: first I must tell my mother where I was. She probably thought it was some childish, adolescent stunt I was pulling, and my aunt didn't want her sister to think I was dead. I thought that maybe Aunt Estelle didn't care. I didn't tell her the whole story, because my mom had forbidden me to.

The next day, my aunt called and spoke to my mother. My aunt told my mother I could live with her and my cousin for now. My mother convinced my aunt that our differences could be resolved and that she wanted to talk to me. She said that I could stay with my aunt if we were unable to work it out; she just wanted to see me first. I begged my Aunt Estelle not to make me go, saying that I couldn't face my mother. Taneasha was very upset and told her mother that they were going to take me back. My aunt assured her that Butch and my mother wouldn't do that. I was so scared. I didn't want to get into trouble; I'd been through enough. It seemed like an eternity in hell as I waited for Mother to come.

Of course, she didn't come alone, either. Butch was with her. Did I expect she might take my running away seriously and actually help me? They finally arrived and said that they wanted to talk to me by myself, that we were going to the mall and we would talk there. That was one bleak car ride.

As we drove, my mother had asked why I was doing this to her. I didn't give her an answer. I just stared at the back of her head and thought, *What do you mean, why am I doing this to you? Shouldn't the question be Why are you doing this to me mom, you are my mother?*

I don't think I processed any more of that conversation into long-term memory. I cannot remember it. Maybe I knew it was all a load of crap and not worth stressing my brain cells over, or perhaps they just could not make me care about what they thought anymore.

On the way to the mall, Butch detoured into an IHOP. My cousin had followed us. Taneasha told them to let me go with her. My stepfather told her it wasn't any of her business as he shoved me back into the car. He said this was a family matter and to butt out. My cousin told my parents off that day, if her body language was any indication. She looked furious as I watched the three of them from the confines of the car. Like me, she was helpless against them. I sat there overcome with hate and fear and lassitude.

I didn't want to go with them, but I was still afraid of disobeying my mother. I can't recall what we talked about on the way home. I was shutting down. I thought I was about to have a nervous breakdown. I couldn't do this anymore. I wanted to be free. Even though I was only fifteen and had no money or job, I would rather have been homeless and to die of frostbite and starvation than to live in their household.

My reverie was interrupted as Butch pulled up to the Berkley Police Station. It was just a small trailer and not an actual building. Butch took me inside because my parents had filed a missing persons report and he needed to tell the police they had found me. I stood there mute and listless as the policeman joked with Butch about the facilities. The dumpy middle aged cop laughed and said that if they had more than two prisoners they would have to handcuff them to each other around a tree outside. Butch roared with laughter. It must be a cop thing because I didn't think it was that funny. The cop turned his beady brown eyes towards me and disgustedly shook his head. "You should not be running away, girlie, it is a dangerous world out there!" the cop lectured. And that was it! He didn't ask me if I were ok or why I had run in the first place. Who exactly was he serving and protecting? Not me! Nobody seemed to find it necessary to protect me. I shuffled back to the car like a zombie. I knew I was alive but that I might as well have been dead.

When we got back, I went downstairs to my room and stayed there. I didn't want to see anyone. I didn't even take care of my siblings. I could no longer do that. I was getting ready to go to bed when my stepfather called me upstairs. I remember laying my head down and praying. My prayer was something like, *Please God, help me, and make him leave me be because I can't take this anymore.* Butch told me he just wanted to talk to me. As I reluctantly but obediently trudged up the stairs, I thought, *I don't want to talk to you or to Mother. I just want to be left alone.*

He was lying on the couch in the living room, and he told me to come over to him. I wouldn't move. Then he said please, and I wanted to just collapse. He told me to come lie on top of him. I was shaking so badly and I remember wanting to vomit as my ears took in the sound of that sickly-sweet, fake voice. But I obeyed him. I laid my body on his because of those awful years of being his plaything and doing what I was told. He told me to relax as I was lying sprawled on top of him, trying to avoid any contact with his crotch. He told me then that he was sorry and that he just wanted to work it out and be a family. He asked if I would give him a second chance. I lied and told him yes. I couldn't say what I really was feeling about how much he scared me physically and had scarred me emotionally. How could I trust him or my mother ever again?

At school the next day, I remembered that I had my cousin's leather jacket. I had to get it back to her and my mother wasn't going to bring it to her, much less let me talk to her again. I asked the teacher if I could go to the guidance counselor's office. The first thing the counselor asked was if I was all right. I told her I was just tired from sleeping over at my cousin's house. I knew I looked a wreck. I had bags under my eyes from lack of sleep all night, and she could see the evidence of that. I told her I needed to call my cousin because I had taken her jacket. The counselor let me.

Taneasha was so happy that I called. She told me that she felt terrible about her mom letting them take me back, but that she had kept her promise not to tell my secret. There was no way I could blame Aunt Estelle for returning me to my mother, so I didn't. Taneasha said that she knew that I would call and that she was coming to get me from wherever I might be calling from. I told her that I was in school and I was calling about her jacket. She said she didn't care about the jacket, just me, and to let her come get me. I told her my mother had said I couldn't leave and my stepfather had promised he would not touch me again, as if that made up for all the times he already had. I really wanted her to come and pick me up, but I was terrified of getting into more trouble. I had never openly defied my parents before now, and life was bad enough at home without any retaliation being added to the mix. Finally she convinced me that I should go with her. I asked how I was going to leave school, since they wouldn't release me to her. She told me not to worry and that she'd deal with that when she got there.

About an hour later, the counselor called me back down to her office, and Taneasha was waiting for me outside the office in the hall. I worried about what we were going to do, but she calmly took my arm and said, "Walk with me out to the car." We began to walk out when she noticed that I didn't have her leather jacket. She told me to get it from my locker. Then she told me to just walk normally: "Walk out the door like you know what you're doing." We went to her car, climbed in, and she sped off. I laughed at her audacity. She'd just swiped me from school without turning a hair. She was like a knight in shining armor charging in on a beautiful, trusty steed, only she was just a girl driving an old, brown Chevy Corsica. I had definitely called in the right troops regardless of the mode of transport—all one of them. Taneasha acted like an invading army of one, ready to save my day.

She turned to me as we drove away and gave me that beautiful, wolfish grin. She knew she'd done good! We laughed and high-fived as my heart cheered for my freedom!

As we headed away from Bristol Plymouth and my hometown, Taneasha told me I was going to have to stay at another house so my mother and stepfather couldn't find me. She brought me to Aunt Beatrice in nearby Randolph. Aunt Beatrice was really my second cousin. She was much older, and out of respect I had always called her Aunt BeBe.

Taneasha had told her of my past against my wishes, but with good reason. I hadn't seen much of Aunt BeBe in the past ten years, and I wasn't real comfortable around her when we got there. She could tell that and made a big effort to make me feel welcome. That first night at Aunt BeBe's house, we didn't talk about what had gone on at my home. She just petted and fussed over me instead, gave me the pull-out couch to sleep on, and I gratefully stayed with her and her family for months.

In the ensuing weeks, she let me battle my demons for myself until she knew it was time to throw down the gauntlet and wage war for me. She waited until I was ready to accept the help she was willing to give, which would eventually provide to me my retribution.

The only things I truly missed from my home were my little sister and two baby brothers. I was feeling bored because I no longer had the responsibilities of bathing them, making up their bottles, or putting them to sleep. I had pretty much raised them like my own and they'd been my security blanket from the cold reality of the abuse I'd endured. I was hurting terribly from the separation and I wondered often how they were faring without me.

As I look back on that time in my life, most of it is only a hazy recollection. My psyche seems to have filtered things out and determined what it's allowed me to retain despite years of psychological examination and therapy. I have had to reconstruct much of this period of my life through conversations with the loving part of my extended family that navigated me through the vortex of emotions that constituted my life from the ages of fifteen through eighteen. Those relatives held their memories of those years close and waited until I was ready to hear them. I am thankful to them for their stewardship of my memories.

I couldn't be enrolled in school because I didn't have the proper paperwork, so I started going with my aunt during the day to the school where she was a first-grade teacher. She explained my predicament to the principal, who permitted me to volunteer in a kindergarten classroom until a solution to my situation could be found. When surrounded by those kindergarteners in that happy, colorful, bright classroom, I was able to repress the pain of losing all my siblings.

I was always very good with children, and as such I thoroughly enjoyed my time at Aunt BeBe's school and felt at peace there. I loved being surrounded by children who gave their love unconditionally and who didn't judge me, but who instead just accepted me for who I was. They wanted love and attention, period. I think those kids acted as a sort of balm for my wounded heart.

The teacher I was assigned to was wonderful, and I think she was amazed by how good I was with the children. One day she asked me if I knew of anything that would motivate the children to be tidy. I had the perfect thing. I had watched so many children's movies and shows over the years with my siblings, and yet the first thing that came to mind was the *Barney* TV show. A song was sung at the end of each episode: the "Clean Up" song. I began singing it to the children. The lyric was: *Clean up, clean up, Everybody everywhere.* The children began to clean up with smiles on their faces. The teacher loved the way I was able to gain the children's attention. She bought a *Barney* CD and used it in her classroom every day from then on.

Eventually, Aunt BeBe let it be known that she was concerned about me not attending school. We had finally talked about what my stepfather had done and we needed to get things arranged so that she could be my temporary guardian.

My parents would have to turn over my school records, and I wanted to get a restraining order against my stepfather. He had promised me that he would never touch me again, but I wanted some recourse if he even came near me. I had a hard enough time being around any strange males now, and it would destroy me completely if I were forced to be in his general vicinity. My aunt and her sisters were ready to wage that war for me now, because I was ready to let them. The courts granted me a temporary restraining order — a small victory, since it was only good for about ten days.

I was taken to a doctor to whom I had to explain that I had been sexually abused. I was given what I refer to as (and what I remember telling myself was) a sex exam. The whole process was embarrassing. How degraded I felt sitting there in that sterile gown, mortified by what was being done in the examination room. I'd obviously never been to the gynecologist, being so young. The stirrups, metal tools, and sharp swabs felt overwhelmingly invasive. My cousin Raia held my hand the whole time and whispered verbal support in my ear. She always seemed to be taking me to doctors' appointments. This one was by far the worst. I would not have survived the humiliation without her support.

They drew my blood for testing to make sure I hadn't contracted AIDS or anything else, and to determine if I might be pregnant. I remember all those years praying I wouldn't get pregnant. If I was the least bit late with my period, I would punch my stomach until it was battered and bruised. The weird thing is, I understood and appreciated abortion in principle, but would've balked at killing a child, even if it had been Butch's seed planted in me by rape. Yet I still couldn't stand the thought of having his child. Talk about a moral conundrum. Thankfully, God spared me any need to make such a decision.

I was asked so many questions, and I believe my questioners went out to my parents' house to visit the other children to make sure they weren't being hurt. I told them I didn't believe any of the other children were being abused, because they were his kids. I was the only one who wasn't his biological child.

It had become a mission for the loving part of my family to make Butch pay for his sins. Nobody was willing to wait and let God sort him out. He needed to pay, then and there on mortal ground, or so we believed. I had to go in front of a judge at the Supreme Court of Massachusetts to give evidence in the indictment of my stepfather. I had to testify against him with his overpowering presence there before me and in front of my mother and stepsisters while being watched by strangers.

It was torturous being in that fancy room, and I was overwhelmed by everything that was about to happen. It wasn't a huge courtroom such as you see on TV, but smaller and more intimate. The furniture was a golden-colored wood that reminded me of honey, so soft and gooey and sweet, and not like the mean pieces of furniture in the rooms where I was forced to receive oral sex and endure hard, searing rape.

Walking to my seat with my family clustered near became a daunting task as I spied Butch and Mother sitting in the "enemy" section. They were so close by after months of us being separated, and yet a chasm of guilt and betrayal yawned between us. I had to walk alone to the witness chair. The judge was speaking, but I was not really able to take in much of what he was saying.

I clung onto the edge of the black swivel chair by the side of the judge's platform, all primed for flight like a bird startled and needing escape. My heart threatened to beat its way out of my chest and my breath seemed to desert me altogether. I stared across the abyss and was mesmerized by the thought that Butch was the only father figure I had had. My mother's unfailing support for him shook my convictions. Would anybody ever really believe me? Couldn't I just forget it all and never have to face him again? Mom was wearing her favorite purple ensemble, and he was draped in the suit he'd worn for our family portrait. His mismatched eyes were shrouded by mirrored sunglasses.

The judge couldn't even guess how afraid I was of Butch. I felt like a timid little rabbit stuck in a snare with a ravenous, snarling wolf bearing down on it, jowls streaming spit and with blood in its eyes. The judge began to understand after he had spoken softly to me several times and yet I remained frozen and couldn't talk. I tore my eyes from my parents in self-defense and nearly swooned from lack of air; then I caught the judge's eyes. They were very bright, with understanding and sympathy shining from within. I could at least see that. He told me to look at him, to look only at him, and to pretend that there was no one else in the courtroom.

I stared at him, completely mesmerized by the compassion I felt coming from him, and I finally began to talk. There was no embellishment, no exaggeration, just the burning truth. I was deaf to the anguish voiced by my commiserating supporters and slandering detractors. I told the judge everything from the very beginning: the first lesson with the disgusting, toothless kiss, the second lesson of orgasm by oral sex Butch had taught to me for years, and the last lesson of rape, which he subjected me to in the ensuing years of my childhood. No more could lies and prevarication haunt me. At last, the real truth, the whole truth, and nothing but the truth, was out. After the recitation of this, my sexual initiation and education, I left the courtroom and was led into a room with my aunts and cousin—a room where I wanted to curl up into a ball and die.

I don't remember if I was granted the permanent restraining order or whether he was indicted. All I know is that my mother and stepfather, at long last, left me alone. I guess they became embarrassed and gave my aunts the necessary paperwork and documents so that I could return to school.

I was told much later that my mother stood up in court and called me a liar in defense of her husband. There was no shock, no hate, no misunderstanding, just nothing. She needed him to support her and the kids, and I was something like a fifth wheel at that point. To her, I didn't matter much more than those cigarettes she'd pitched in the trash when I had lied for her. I understood why she wouldn't fight for me, since to her and to Butch, I was expendable. It was the final nail in my psychological coffin. It was then that I lost my mind!

I was now embroiled in the second fight for my life. I'd survived premature birth, jaundice, and low birth weight the first time, but this time I now understood that I was in serious mental trouble and I didn't care at all. Part of me didn't want to live. It was as simple as that. I spent over six months in psychiatric wards following several attempts at suicide, hospital stays, and couch surfing in the homes of relatives and dropping out of school. I was mortally depressed.

My stepfather may well have raped my body, but the desecration of my mind, my heart, and my soul was far more destructive. Over the next two years, I drove my loving, supporting adoptive family crazy. My mom had certainly let me down emotionally, but boy, her sisters, my Aunt BeBe, and my cousins picked up the slack and did their best to help me put the pieces back together.

This was done against staggering odds. I was perceived to be insane and diagnosed as bipolar and suicidal. Lord, I don't know how they stood me as long as they did. Talk about guessing who was coming to dinner! I was manic-depressive and acted like I had multiple personality disorder; they never knew who I'd be or what I'd do next — then again, neither did I!

Going back to school, it was clear that I had issues. My aunts had put me in therapy where I was diagnosed with severe depression and post-traumatic stress disorder. I was constantly having flashbacks about the abuse and its aftermath, and the flashbacks caused debilitating panic attacks. I couldn't sleep at night. I was afraid of the dark, just like a small child. I didn't want to live, but I didn't really want to die, either. I was out of the situation, but with all the traumas I had experienced at Butch's hands, I was a basket case.

One day I overdosed on my prescription medication and tried to slice open my wrist. Thankfully, I was too doped up to be effective with the knife, and the cut was superficial. In the emergency room, I wouldn't drink the antidote, the charcoal cocktail, so I was tied down and a tube was shoved down my throat to administer that milky, grey liquid. My stomach had to be pumped. That really sucked. The procedure felt like some huge monster clawing its way down my throat, grabbing my stomach, and with a crushing grip contracting my guts and forcing a geyser of burning bile and acid laced with drugs to spew out of my ravaged throat. After that lovely experience, my wrist was bandaged and when physicians knew I was physically OK, they put me in a psychiatric ward on a seventy-two-hour hold where all the patients were young adults facing their own demons.

This became a pattern for me. I didn't cut myself anymore, but I was still screaming for attention. The relatives were trying to help, but they had their own families to contend with, plus their jobs and other worries. My mother's family was overwhelmed by all the help I needed. There were threats of kidnapping charges from my stepfather when they initially hid me. There were months of angst in dealing with my nightmares. There were court appearances, several suicide attempts, and hospitalizations. All this had tapped out their strength. I continue to love them deeply for all they did and tried to do, and I vowed I would never again be a burden to them.

Much, much later I learned that my real dad's family had been searching for me for years. They had tried to reach out to me. It was Butch who had blocked their efforts to locate me. He wouldn't communicate with them in any way. They continued to wonder what had become of little Kathryn Harriet Muhammad.

When I finally reached out to them, my biological father's family waded into the battle to save Katie. I stayed with my Auntie Betty for a while and for a short time with my paternal grandmother. Having me in her house had to rock my grandma's ordered, dictatorial soul to the ground. I was just too much for her. I tried to kill myself again.

This latest attempt to take my life landed me in Belmont's McLean Hospital, a renowned psychiatric facility. It was the best hospital I ever woke up in. The other hospitals were just trying to keep me from dying and didn't deal with any underlying issues. At McLean I was placed in the lockdown unit for about two weeks. Even though I didn't want to, I had to talk about the abuse. Yes, the sexual abuse had been monumental, but it was the pain arising from the fact that my mother never fought on my behalf that was insurmountable.

In time, I was transferred into what is called the residential program where we were only locked up at night. I remained there for about a month. Each day, I had about six hours of group and individual therapy. I worked one on one with a therapist, and the psychiatrist responsible for me prescribed medications for my depression, the panic attacks, my bipolar condition, and post-traumatic stress disorder. Anyone who has been through that kind of intensive psychiatric upheaval will tell you, or at least would think it to themselves, that hours a day of intensive therapy is no joyride.

For instance, in group therapy, you and your fellow patients are clustered in a room lacking any adornment or distractions. There's just chairs and coffee and blank walls. It's dull and clinical. A sterile environment perhaps describes it best. Let's face it, you aren't there for any sightseeing, not externally anyway. There's nothing to look at except the inside of you.

Every story told in group therapy is worse than the previous one, and you can comprehend that the pain of the others in the group is as bad as yours, if not more so. Nevertheless, it is all still extremely personal and one-sided. Every time I was encouraged to speak about my situation, I'd break into a sweat. Each retelling felt like a surgical procedure with no anesthesia; every question was like a scalpel slicing into my psyche. The incisions cut deep and long into my memory and emotions. The excisions dragged the blood and gore of my humiliation out into the open to be studied and diagnosed by onlookers. It was enlightening and it was healing, but still, it hurt like hell! Who knew you had to be gutted before there'd be a chance to rebuild yourself?

When I was released I was hardly cured, but I no longer dwelt on thoughts of suicide. After I left the hospital, my family knew that it would be an impossible task to continue trying to deal with all my issues and carry on with their lives in a normal manner. Together we decided that the next step was for me to transition into a teenage-centered shelter.

The place wasn't bad. I could hide in plain sight with plenty of company around. I attended my prescribed therapy, kept to myself, and survived. I was a junior in high school, but I dropped out because I was so far behind in my studies that I was flunking everything. It wasn't that I was stupid. I was just overwhelmed and emotionally incapable of sitting in class with classmates whose only worry was what their dates would be like over the weekend. It seemed I was traveling fast on a bad track to nowhere.

One afternoon, a visitor came to see me at the shelter. She was an older person and a family friend. I had been boycotting any family visits so they wouldn't be forced to disown me. Auntie Betty, my real dad's sister, had a very dear friend who had been sexually abused. Her name was Marilyn. Betty asked her friend to visit me.

Marilyn ignored my boycott, my means of avoiding burdening anybody anymore, and she barreled right into my life big-time. She tiptoed around my finer feelings for about five seconds before I knew she was a force to be reckoned with. She was decidedly straightforward and very supportive. For me, she was the right person at the right time.

With Marilyn's help, I could see a better future. She pulled me off my course of self-destruction, dragged me away from the bad track where I had been derailed for such a long time, and blasted me with her honesty. Her solution was really simple. It was something like a demented dare. Either I could get up, stop being depressed, and turn my life around, or I could accept things as I perceived them to be and do nothing but shut up and stagnate forever. Marilyn demanded that I make the decision to grow up and become an independent woman with a will to succeed and not just a will to live. She then made a commitment to me not to shy away. She knew that my treacherous climb up a huge mountain of pain would be difficult, because there was a time when she had had to do it for herself. She wasn't going to coddle me. Marilyn made it clear that she would not carry me or my load. I had to toil alone.

For weeks on end, this family friend badgered me, then helped me, to get my GED (General Equivalency Diploma). Once that was accomplished, she forced me to enroll in the local community college. I did all this while continuing to live in the teen shelter. I actually received the high school equivalency quite a bit earlier than if had I stuck it out in high school and graduated. That fact made me extremely proud and underpinned the beginnings of a newfound sense of self.

I have thought of Marilyn fondly and frequently since those days when she helped my indomitable will to live resurface and guided me to the decision to excel rather than to just survive. She opened my eyes and my heart to new emotions and helped me to truly believe in myself. I thank her from the bottom of my heart and from the center of my soul!

For all my supportive family who put up with me those ghastly two years, there are really no appropriate words that I can use to express my feelings and my thanks. They know how grateful I am. Where would I have ended up without them?

4. Summiting the Mountain

Somehow I had survived some of the worst years a young girl could be forced to endure, thanks to the aid of some wonderful family members and a family friend. As related in the last chapter, I was far from cured when released from McLean Hospital, but I came away from there knowing how much I was in need of psychological assistance. I was willing to accept help, and with my eyes wide open, I pursued therapy full throttle.

The true beginning of my advancement toward recovery must have occurred as I struggled for my GED. Marilyn, the family friend who'd prodded me unmercifully to accomplish that feat, became even more determined in her efforts to propel me into higher education. I had always felt safest away from my stepfather when I was in school and away from my living nightmare, so it should not come as a surprise that I truly was not reluctant to go. I was eager but terrified I'd fail Marilyn and my family.

My new life in a community college began much as it does for any student with financial worries, a lack of opportunity, and a preponderance of lust. I wanted to fit in like a typical student, so I pretended that I didn't need a job and applied for financial aid. I also started dating, finally. The financial aid came through, there didn't seem to be any jobs for me anyway, and dating a few guys was OK until I remembered that I really did not like men.

It wasn't the fault of the guys I dated. It was Butch's fault. He was the last guy I was around with any regularity, and he had burnt all their bridges for them with all his lessons. I just didn't want to be with any males during my free time, especially since I hadn't preferred men to begin with.

I remembered my dream about kissing a girl and liking it at about the same time I met the one person who ignited a spark of attraction. Her name was Barbara. She was attending a workshop at a local woman's center. I had signed up too late to attend the workshop for my age group and ended up with the older women. Barbara and I had an immediate emotional connection. Wow!

She and I started hanging out together, which was great, and she began helping me with college work by studying with me. It didn't take long before I found out that Barbara was smart right down to the ground, truly brilliant, especially compared to how I felt about myself. Within six months, we had an apartment and were living together. For the first time in my life, I was sharing expenses, time, and feelings with someone. The best part was that it was my decision to do so.

I'd sit over my books in our tiny world and stare at her in disbelief. She was pretty in an unassuming way. She had quiet manners and a rather sad smile. She had also experienced emotional pain in her life. I felt overcome by her acceptance of my past and was able to grow healthier psychologically because of her nurturing spirit.

We were poor but happy. I transferred to Boston University, where she was studying. Barbara was my biggest cheerleader, teacher, and friend. She was eleven years my senior, and she became my life partner.

When she was young, Barbara had been diagnosed with rheumatoid arthritis. By the time we met, the arthritis had begun to take an emotional and physical toll on her. The constant, aching pain became almost unbearable because of the winters in Massachusetts.

She had been applying for jobs in schools located in warmer climates and was offered a position in Florida. Here I was, feeling settled, and I had finally found someone who loved me unconditionally — and she was going to leave. Barbara asked me to go with her. Could I desert all my roots? It was a dilemma for me whether I should move to Florida with Barbara or stay behind and be alone again. Though I had not been permitted to see my siblings much, I would still miss them terribly were I to leave. I even missed my stepsisters, who'd severed all contact when I was forced to lie about their dad and they had even blamed me for his unexpected death. I had really had no communication with the rest of my family either, since I had been such a burden to them. Was there really a reason to stay in Boston?

We decided to move. The warmer weather would help Barbara's arthritis, and I could turn a new page in my life. It was exciting and scary at the same time. Although I had travelled a great deal as a child with my paternal relatives, I had never ventured far from Boston with my mother and stepfather. I was about to move to a place as different from my home as milk was to vinegar.

We landed in Palm Beach County, which is north of Fort Lauderdale in Broward County and about sixty miles north of Miami. The town of Palm Beach was (and remains) a world unto its own, but the rest of the county is fairly laid back. There was a small-hometown atmosphere. It was sun drenched and at times sweaty, but nothing compares to the calming, gentle breezes that flow incessantly through the swaying palm trees. I loved it!

When we first moved down, I continued with my education and took a job in construction. Construction wasn't what I really wanted to do; I wanted to work with children. Barbara knew how much I loved children, so she suggested I start a family daycare. Boy, did she live to regret that sound advice.

The idea that I could create a pre-school galvanized everything within me. I was immediately and completely consumed with ambition. I had a goal! Here was a chance to do what I loved and something that I had known about my whole life! I would take care of children and save them from the emotional and physical starvation I had endured as a young girl. What a wonderful idea! I was no longer buried underneath my emotions. I was suddenly scaling the base of my mountainous grief, and the summit was in sight.

A local shop owner in Lake Worth, where we lived, had befriended Barbara and me. Andy owned several businesses, and I planted myself down in his presence and began picking his brain. Poor guy! I was tireless in my pursuit to create a company. Thankfully, he was a good sport. He took me by the hand and led me through the maze of private incorporation, tax strategies, and all the little details of owning a business. Andy was a godsend. I am forever grateful to him.

The Palm Beach County Health Department is where you have to go to collect the necessary paperwork and manuals required to open a family daycare. While waiting for the county's approval of my application, I studied the rules and regulations mandated for pre-schools. I was a great student. My ADHD did not deter me from meandering through the myriad little quirks of the system. I learned everything I needed to know. I was going to do this right.

Katie's Kids Learning Center was incorporated in November 2003. My hearing for approval of licensure with the health department was slated for the following February. I was ready for whatever they asked of me.

During the interim, I became acquainted with Family Central. This is an organization that helps with funding for families in financial crisis. The Department of Children and Families, a branch of the Department of Health, could also intervene and place children with Family Central if there were concerns about a child's welfare at home. This was right up my alley. This was the nucleus of the very group of children I wanted to help. They were poor, disenfranchised, and in some cases abused, just like me.

Barbara and I had bought a small house in Lake Worth with money she'd earned during a teaching stint in Japan. My biological father came down from Massachusetts to help me redo our little home. This was the first time in ages we'd spent one-on-one

time together. It was nerve wracking! I wanted him there helping me, but his psychological demons and my new personality clashed. I truly do not know who was more screwed up. At
times we laughed ourselves into hysterics as we worked away.
Sometimes it seemed that I was speaking Earthling to his Martian!
Nevertheless, I love my dad and I let nothing else matter.

The house turned out beautifully, but not without some blood,
sweat, and tears. It became a wonderful place to raise other people's children. As I stood alone one day appreciating my efforts,
it dawned on me that the house and I were a lot alike. Our house
had to be gutted to make it whole again, just as I had been at
McLean Hospital. I'd torn out all the nasty dark parts and filled
the void with new light ones. It dawned on me that I had just
taken a colossal leap up my mountain of pain, and I was climbing
toward the summit and complete healing.

When I finally opened the welcoming doors to our home, I
operated as a seven-day-a-week, twenty-four-hour-a-day family
pre-school. I did this because some of the parents didn't work a
traditional nine-to-five job. Although it wasn't really cost-effec-
tive, because I only had a couple of children at night and through
the weekends, I was trying to help the parents who needed the
support of a twenty-four-hour childcare so that they could go to
work and not worry about what to do with their little ones when
their schedule gave them odd hours.

I was to be the super caregiver who would shield all my children from loneliness, neglect, and abuse. I wanted to protect
them as if they were my very own. Closer to the truth, though, I
wanted to protect them and live my lost childhood through them.

With the pre-school in our house, Barbara was totally overwhelmed by my absorption in the kids. She could never come
home and relax because I had children in the house constantly.
Therefore, the two of us began speaking different languages, too,
and neither of us bothered to interpret what the other was saying. This communication breakdown lasted the whole first year.

In one therapeutic, all-encompassing argument, Barbara
finally talked, and I listened. She put it this way: she would no
longer have strange children invading our bed, reliving their

nightmares. She couldn't and wouldn't accept a sink full of Cheerio-encrusted bowls and coagulating sippy cups. She refused to comfort our dog when kids tried to shove crayons up his poor butt, and she wouldn't use a bathroom disgustingly adorned by little boys learning to point their equipment. She wanted them out of our house. I couldn't blame her for a moment.

Barbara was bowled over by my passionate pursuit of this dream. She knew of my abuse but was unprepared for my singular, burning desire to help kids in want. She couldn't comprehend how I chose to hide behind them. She didn't understand that if I made them happy, then my own sorry existence, my past, no longer mattered. I began to blend in with the children, and my life blurred at the edges. As if by osmosis, I was melting through barriers and becoming one with my kids. It felt like I was healing. But was I?

We finally decided that we should open a real pre-school in a separate location. It was a big move with scary financial implications. It would be fine as long as all my ill-mannered brats were anywhere but in our home. We didn't even discuss my personal investment in the proposed venture, though. I always seem to get lost a bit in the shuffle.

We chose a school in nearby Boynton Beach that was already running so that we could immediately redirect children to the new facility. We bought it in July of 2005 by mortgaging our home and referred to it as "Boynton."

My dear dad came flying in to the rescue to give me a hand fixing up the building. The miscommunications and personality conflicts we'd had before were multiplied by the size of the project, but we muddled and laughed our way through. I had never appreciated my dad as much as when we were slaving over some knotty construction problem, such as where to cut the holes in the drywall for sockets and switches. Try doing that with a kooky relative when you are nuts yourself and see how well you do. It gives sanity a whole new meaning. But once again, I got to tear out some of the bad stuff in myself and insert some good.

The former owner of the pre-school stayed on for a couple of months to help with the transition. I loved those days. I was climbing harder toward fulfillment, and happiness and my goals were in sight.

I became a hands-on owner who wouldn't ask staff to do anything that I wouldn't do. I loved the children so much that I would teach the volunteer prekindergarten (VPK) class every year, at least at the beginning, to get acquainted with my young charges. I wanted to make sure the children would walk out of the pre-school and be qualified for advanced placement when they left Katie's Kids Learning Center. I would always tell the staff that if the children were to someday work at McDonald's, then I wanted them to be a CEO!

I placed high expectations on the children. Normally, by the end of pre-K, they were doing second-grade work. So many of the children would later tell their parents that the regular public school work was so much easier than what they had been expected to do at the pre-school.

I loved these children so much. I was always buying the most expensive, high-tech educational materials and toys I could get my hands on. I wanted these children to have better chances than any of the rich kids. In life, you have the haves and the have-nots. I didn't want my children to be the forgotten ones. I didn't want to produce any have-nots. I wanted them to have the best tools available so that they could embrace great opportunities. I wanted to be them, so I lived as them.

Some of their parents were being monitored by the Department of Children and Families (DCF), the state regulatory body affiliated with the Department of Health that acts as a watchdog for children in underprivileged families or anywhere abuse is suspected. The DCF would determine if the children were in a safe environment. If they were not, DCF had the power to remove children from their custodians whether they were parents, grandparents, or other relatives.

The DCF families often had problems feeding their children and paying their rent, their water bills, and even their electric bills. They never sent the kids to pre-school with any diapers other than the ones they were already wearing, and they never packed them lunches. I paid many of their bills and would drop off food to these families. (You can be sure that if I never make macaroni and cheese again, it'll still be too soon.) I bought shipments of diapers: vans full to the ceiling. It impressed my employees, and frustrated them as well. They thought I was far too giving. They didn't understand my depth of involvement with these children. Depriving them would be depriving me.

Barbara couldn't grasp what had happened at all. She thought by removing the kids from our home, she'd have more time with me alone. Instead of that, now I was constantly on the run. There were early transportation pickups, field trips, aftercare hours, late parents, and endless business duties, all of which kept me away. She couldn't understand what took so much of my time. Even when I was home, I couldn't stop worrying about my kids.

One day when Barbara came to visit me at the school, an aftercare student came to the office, grabbed me by the arm, and said, "Miss Katie, you know that this is the weekend, don't you? If I'm not here, I don't know when I'll eat again." Barbara looked pained and confused. She was sorry for the child and curious why I was being told about there being no food at home. When the child asked, "Can you please drop off food to our house again? Please, please, please." My Barbara watched me and waited for my response. I knelt down and hugged the child and promised to bring some food to the house. I gave a kiss and back to class the child went. Barbara gave me that sad smile as it dawned on her that I was in way over my head with these kids. I was contributing much more than anyone else would have, and it wasn't likely I'd stop.

Until now, Barbara had been unaware of my extracurricular spending. It wasn't that I thought she would begrudge the kids anything, only that the expense had become so much that she would naturally want to have a say. She was my partner, after all. Yet I wasn't going to let anybody steer me away from my intentions.

There was the time when one of my DCF mothers called me at work. She was frantic. She pleaded with me to come over right away and help her because the DCF was there and the cops would soon be coming. She was about to lose her children again because she didn't have adequate food supplies. She was a loving mother—truthfully, better than most—but she was very poor. Her children were always clean and presentable, with good manners and easy ways. They may not have had brand names on all their clothes, but they always looked well turned out. They displayed to the world how much she cared about them. They were a reflection of their loving mother. I dropped what I was doing and drove to the grocery store, where I spent about three hundred dollars on provisions. I then had to race to get to the parent's house before the authorities took the children away. I hauled the groceries in from the car and placed them on the counter.

The DCF worker asked me why I was doing this. I told her that if I didn't do it, then no one else would. I explained that I cared about the children and didn't care about the money. I was in this field of work because I loved the children. The caseworker asked me for my number and I gave her my card. She gave me hers in return. I told her she was welcome to call me at any time, and if she wanted, I could keep her updated on any children about whom I might have concerns. I was so empowered that day that I felt like a superhero, only one in regular clothes.

Walking into my pre-school every day brought me so much joy. It lifted my spirits, because it helped me forget my own lingering depression and the past from which I had come. When I walked into any of the schools that we came to operate, I was treated like a rock star. All the children, no matter what they were doing, would jump up and give me the biggest hugs. I would sit with them and ask them how they were doing, and I'd make a point of really listening to what they had to say. I'd read to them or engage in any activity they were doing. Every child who walked into my schools over the seven years that I owned them stole a piece of my heart.

A lot of these children were living in poverty. If I had not arranged funding for their attendance, courtesy of the Early Learning Coalition, they wouldn't have been there at all. In our pre-care and aftercare programs, many of the older ones would've been left to their own devices, alone at home or possibly out wandering the streets. We accepted children from infancy to age thirteen. I felt it was paramount that my facilities provide a safe place for these youngsters when their parents were working and unavailable.

I remember one precious little boy for whom I had to make sure I had extra food every day. The pre-schools were on the food program, funded by Family Central. We provided the students with a free daily breakfast, lunch, and a snack. One day the staff was cleaning the tables and I noticed this child finding his way to wherever there were leftovers, trying to eat them all up before they were thrown away. It wasn't the foster parent's fault, but this child had been neglected. He would try to eat as much as he could possibly get his hands on. His biological parents hadn't fed him as much as they should have, and this had become his coping mechanism to make sure that he would never be hungry again. Consequently, he gorged himself whenever food was around. It reminded me of when my stepsister sneaked out of the bedroom window and loaded us all up on crabapples because we were hungry a lot when our parents were broke. We'd invariably get tummy aches, but at least we were full for a time.

Every child has his or her own story, and I knew there were many more children who needed my help. I was determined to help as many as I possibly could.

In October of 2006, I bought the biggest facility I would ever own. It was in a predominately upper-middle-class section of Margate, which is west of Pompano Beach and a fair distance south of Boynton, Lake Worth, and West Palm Beach. I called it Wexford Academy, doing business as a subsidiary of Katie's Kids Learning Center.

How could I forget those first days after I bought Margate? I put every penny I had into buying the building. At the closing, I received a check back from the bank that I used as startup capital to pay the bills. When I left the closing and everything was in place, I found that I didn't have any cash to pay the toll to get back to West Palm Beach! I didn't know we were going to take the turnpike, so I called the broker on his cell to inform him I had no money with me. The broker had to pay from his car, which was ahead of mine. When we got back to West Palm, he bought lunch too. Here I was, buying a $2.4 million piece of real estate, and I didn't have ten dollars to my name, let alone in my pocket.

Margate was a much bigger school than Boynton and had a totally different racial demographic. I was praying that I would be able to fill the school quickly, because we were short more than thirty students—who represented over twenty thousand dollars per month in needed revenue. My job was cut out for me. The place was huge: I was permitted to have up to a hundred fifty students. Yes, I could help so many more kids, but unfortunately, I would be seeing even less of Barbara now and burying myself deeper in my new family psyche.

I remember meeting the staff for the first time. I was really nervous, because I knew the director was already furious with me; she had also wanted to buy the school. I couldn't help that a hurricane had destroyed the condo she owned and had planned to use as collateral. Of course it wasn't my fault, but she still was angry. It wasn't a very cordial way for us to begin our relationship.

The assistant director, on the other hand, was really nice. She and the director stayed with me after the end of the school day to introduce me to the intricacies and the foibles of Margate. The previous owner had actually been the real estate broker through whom I had bought it, and they told me that he had been an absentee pre-school owner and was never around. The director was accustomed to enjoying her freedom, so she wasn't thrilled to hear me say that I intended to be a hands-on owner. We bumped heads a lot, but I think she grew to appreciate my presence, especially when a bus driver didn't show or some other problem occurred. I took good care of what was mine, including the students, the facility, and my staff.

I remember getting the first bills a month after taking over Margate. I was a stickler for making sure we pared the bills down at Boynton, but here the student population was nearly four times the size. I figured that any funds we saved on the monthly utility bills, something we could surely control, would mean more money for the children.

What a shock I had when I opened that first electric bill and saw that it was well over seven hundred dollars. I nearly fell on the floor. I sucked it up and opened the water bill. It was five hundred and fifty dollars, another enormous amount. Oh, Lord, what was going on? I wondered if people were just going to school there or were living there. I thought that this couldn't possibly be right. Then I opened the waste management bill. That was another six hundred I owed. What did the staff think? That I had planted a money tree? Was it flourishing somewhere in the playground?

The first utility I called was the electric company. I told them there was a huge problem with the bill. The person on the line laughed and said that the monthly amount had decreased considerably since I had taken over the school. Be that as it may, I corralled the directors together and asked them if they had left the air-conditioning running at night and whether the interior lights were being left on. They all looked at me as if I'd asked if the Easter Bunny was staying there. I was somewhat relieved when they said they did leave the AC and the lights on. I told them, "You won't be doing that anymore." I asked them to please be sure to turn off the air-conditioning every night, along with all the lights, to see if we could reduce the electric bill.

Then I went on to the water bill. I was aware of the kids' bathroom habits and knew they tended to forget to flush half the time. So I went into every bathroom to see if there were any problems. I immediately noticed that every toilet in the building was running and that some of the sink faucets were dripping. Why hadn't I noticed this earlier? I called our handyman; he changed out the guts in the toilets and tightened up the faucets. Problem fixed!

Then it was waste management's turn. I noticed that the garbage wasn't full every week, yet we had a huge dumpster that was being picked up twice a week. I called the garbage company and asked them to reduce the size of the dumpster and to only pick up once a week. The director assured me that this wasn't really a very good idea. I said we should try it for a couple of weeks. Guess who was right? Not me! The smaller dumpster, picked up once a week, wasn't big enough, especially considering all the leftover food from the breakfasts and lunches we served the kids.

One Monday, at what turned out to be the end of my trash experiment, I was driving onto the lot and saw the director outside with her pant legs hiked up, no shoes on, and looking completely flabbergasted. I didn't think this was a good sign, especially since she had always worn what looked like expensive clothes and shoes, and she was always so composed. I was a little apprehensive trying to deduce what was happening with her.

In hysterics, she lambasted me. Her prim person was positively quivering with pent-up fury. She screamed at me that since I had been the brilliant one who had the garbage pickup switched to only once a week, I was the one who would have to deal with all the maggots that had infested the dumpster. What a sight! There were maggots everywhere! It's awful to describe such a pulsing, writhing mass of slinky, little white bodies. All along the five-foot high dumpster enclosure and oozing down the dumpster itself was a blanket of stinking fly larvae. It smelled so bad. There must have been billions of them. I gagged and heaved at the visual and olfactory overload. I can be extremely subject to obsessive compulsive disorder (OCD), and I don't do bugs. It was so disgusting that I can't imagine why I didn't just faint.

Being the hands-on owner that I was, I tottered away from my car, grinding my teeth and pretending that I really wanted to help the director. She was still very angry with me, but when I began to help spray the maggots and sweep up the all the remains, she was decidedly more appreciative, especially since I was retching the whole time, eyes streaming and gasping for oxygen like some landed fish.

A couple of times a maggot got on me and I'd screech in hysterics, running around like a chicken with its head cut off, flailing my arms and legs trying to dislodge the thing. The cleanup became quite a show. The director and assistant director were getting a real big laugh watching my antics, at least until the director scooped up a dustpan full of dead creepy crawlies and tripped, dropping the putrid heap on her own bare foot. I can guarantee you, there is not a siren on the planet designed to be heard for miles around that could wail louder than she did. The assistant director and I fell together, clinging to one another for support, frenzied with laughter, camouflaging our distinct thankfulness that this hadn't happened to either of us! After that episode, the three of us were much closer. They knew I was in this for the long haul and would do anything to make it work.

So it was back to the drawing board to figure out how to save on the trash haulage expenses. I refused to pay six hundred dollars a month for garbage collection, but any price was almost worth it if it meant that I would never have another mother of all maggot infestations to clean up. From then on, we used the smaller dumpster but had a twice-a-week pickup. This worked out better, but from time to time I still had to get into the dumpster and jump on all the cardboard and papers it contained to make room for more garbage. Parents and neighbors who saw me jumping up and down in the middle of the dumpster must have thought I was a real oddball! Little did they know that between the garbage, the water, and the electric, I had saved the pre-school about nine hundred dollars a month.

With the bills for the Boynton and Margate pre-schools adding up to about sixty-five thousand a month, nine hundred mightn't seem like a great deal, but it helped me to buy extra supplies and enrichments for the children — things their families couldn't afford.

Once I was settled into a routine, my good dad returned again to Florida to help me redo Margate. All hilarity aside, we produced a beautiful school. It took months of nights and weekends for us to complete the renovation. Margate was a state-of-the-art facility, far surpassing any other pre-school for miles around. Not only that, but I was continuing to rebuild myself, tearing out the bad stuff and replacing it with new, the process I'd begun at McLean's.

It was after the purchase of the Margate school that I decided I needed to get myself a commercial driver's license (CDL). That way, I could operate larger transport vehicles, including buses that carried nearly eighty passengers. I wanted to be able to do any job that my staff did. And it would mean that I could drive any Katie's Kids vehicle when a driver called in sick. The big buses are not like the twelve- and fifteen-passenger vans that don't require a commercial license. You have to be thoroughly trained to know how to transport children safely in these monsters.

Whenever I filled in for a driver, the older aftercare kids would be so excited to see me. They'd yell out, "Yes! Miss Katie is driving us," accompanied by fist pumps. I pretended I didn't notice. They really liked me, because I was just a big kid in an adult body and willing to play as hard as they did. When possible, I would accompany them on field trips. If we went skating, I'd be on the rink with them and we'd play tag. The children who were too big for their own britches and thought themselves too badass to play wouldn't initially follow along as I tagged them, but they sure would look up at me and shoot smiles my way as I smiled at them. I would yell, "You're it!" and suddenly all the cool would melt away and the game was on. They would chase me down twice as hard as the little kids, with the biggest smiles and the most painful butt smashes when they fell, until I let them get me. It made my whole heart smile.

I would try to get my kids whatever gadgets they wanted to play with at Katie's Kids for after school. They began to keep track of when the state funding would come in each month. When that day arrived, I would head out to the store to look for everything on their lists.

2008 is when I bought the school we ended up calling Old Delray. All the schools were owned by Katie's Kids Learning Center, so for the staff it was easier to refer to each with a nickname. This school was my third largest. You can guess who helped me get it ready for the students. I really appreciate my dad. He was my go-to guy.

Soon after Old Delray opened, the father of one of the kids, a local businessman, asked me to help him with his daughter. Jim was the owner of an air-conditioning business called Climate Systems and Cooling. He asked me to meet him at Old Delray to see if I would help his daughter.

Little Luna didn't want to go to school. She was having a hard time adjusting to a structured facility. Growing up, her grandmother had always watched and taken care of her. Jim explained that at Luna's previous pre-school, the teacher had yanked her up by the arm and told her to hush. Jim felt that his little girl had been traumatized by that sort of rough treatment. The day that happened, he held his crying daughter in his arms and asked her if she wanted to stay. She quickly said no, and he immediately took her out of that pre-school.

Jim had heard of Katie's Kids through some friends and decided to contact me based upon their recommendations. When he called and explained the situation, I drove from Margate to Delray to meet with him and his daughter. I talked to Luna and assured her that no one would ever put hands on her at my pre-school. Luna had only one request: she didn't want to take any naps! I made eye contact with her father and saw his silent approval.

Just about every morning for three months, I was there for Luna's arrival. I would sit with her and her mother to try to calm her down. I would explain how she was going to meet and play with other little children. After her mother left, I would pick Luna up and play with her for a little while longer. I asked the staff not to make her take naps. Her father would pick her up like clock-work every day, a little after nap time was to start.

Our curriculum was tough, and she hated our homework, but over time, Luna began to feel more at ease as she learned new concepts. She loved her caring teachers, and after a while, her dad didn't have to come early to get her. Jim came back after Luna finished with us and had gone on to kindergarten to tell me that she loved school. He'd asked her why, and she had said it was because the homework at her school was so much easier than at Miss Katie's. She eventually became a straight-A student. I know this because her loving father likes to keep me up to date.

In 2009, a friend told me about a pre-school that was facing foreclosure. She recommended that I contact the agent, so I called him to see if there was a chance that I could buy the school. The agent contacted the bank that held its mortgage and said I would be a good fit for the property. My pre-schools exceeded state standards and operated at full capacity. All this was a plus with the bank.

I was negotiating vigorously for my fourth pre-school just as our national financial crisis was hitting hard. I made a deal with the bank for a two-year lease with a clause allowing me to buy the property once the term was up. I figured I would be able to get financing by then. Why not? I had been extremely successful, with an exemplary track record.

Up until now, I had always flown my dad down for big projects, and we'd spend nights and weekends working away. But the job of readying this school was much too large for just the two of us. I called around and talked to construction contractors to see how much a project of this magnitude would cost. I figured I would probably have had to spend about thirty thousand dollars after demolition. To save expenses, staff from the other locations came over after working with our pre-school and aftercare children all day to help with the demolition. What a way to work off repressed aggression! This went on forever, or so it seemed, but the staff members who helped were in much happier moods during the day despite how hard they had worked after hours.

For years, I was puzzled about why they had seemed happier. The answer didn't become clear until 2012. I was sitting with my best friend April and her kids in a darkened movie theater watching the Marvel Comics movie, *The Avengers*. Anyone familiar with Marvel's *The Incredible Hulk* knows he has some anger issues (the understatement of the century, right?). As the battle for Earth intensifies, Mr. Tony Stark, the brilliant billionaire playboy also known as Iron Man, tells the Hulk to remember to just smash. I may have lost some of the story from my memory, but the thrust of it was that the Hulk finally figured out it is OK to be pissed off sometimes and that you just have to learn when to release tensions—and to appreciate that when you do, you can get into it! When the Hulk eventually meets the bad guy, who thinks he is a god, the resulting scene is epic. The "god" remonstrates the Hulk like a recalcitrant child and the Hulk picks him up and thrashes him about repeatedly, beating him unmercifully into the ground. It was so hysterical! I about peed my pants (and I'm pretty sure my friend actually did). We laughed until well after the scene ended. We were finally shushed by our people seated near us. Even then, we couldn't help tittering. We were reacting like two teenagers who'd seen their first love scene on the big screen.

That's when I understood why it felt so good to demolish walls and toilets and floors after being nice and polite all day to some of the roughest kids in south Florida. It helped my staff externalize some repressed stuff. They'd never hit a kid, but they might dream about it, especially when a naughty little boy spits in a talking teacher's mouth when he knows he has a strep throat and then brags that that's why he did it.

While I may have had the best pre-schools in south Florida, that didn't mean they were filled with model students. A perfect student was a blessing, but I wanted the bad and underrated problem kids who lived in the worst neighborhoods. Those boys and girls would usually work out that I was sincere, but that I was also tougher than they ever might be and was trying to help them. They would mellow somewhat if they wanted to stay at Katie's Kids, especially since they knew that if they were booted out, their spots would be quickly filled. There was a long waiting list for places in my pre-schools.

Some of my favorite memories from that time include those of a tough little brat with a swagger and attitude to match, who was dragged to the school's doorstep by some tiny woman who looked like she couldn't hurt a fly, much less scare one. It was blatantly obvious who was wearing the pants when she twisted that boy's ear as he begged to be readmitted. The staff loved seeing that too, but sometimes, no matter how much the expelled one whined, we just had to take the next child. I wanted the children who demonstrated that they wanted to learn.

Katie's Kids Learning Center was all about the kids, and for the most part, the staff believed in what we were doing. While refurbishing New Delray, we worked nights and weekends for about two months on the things we could do ourselves, working around the contractors and the jobs they had to do.

I spent every dime I had to make this school as beautiful and educationally well equipped as anything around. The staff was really proud of the job we had undertaken and of our results. This project ended up costing over two hundred thousand dollars, maxed out the company's finances, and left Barbara and me swamped in debt. This was very scary for me. I can't imagine how Barbara felt, since she didn't really have a say (or want one).

By now, I was a nervous wreck and wondering if I had spread us all too thin. I had worked tirelessly for over six years to get the company to this point while helping hundreds of kids and their families, not to mention all the staff and their families. We just had to be able to reap the benefits of our labors, didn't we?

This fourth school opened beautifully and ahead of schedule in September of 2009. It had six classrooms with the latest of everything in each, and together they accommodated seventy-eight students. Our teacher-to-student ratio was well above the state average. But New Delray would soon become infamous.

Within three months of our opening, the enrollment reached capacity. All applications were generated by word of mouth. The schools supported those they could in their surrounding neighborhoods, and word got around that we cared. We fed the children, educated them, and even transported them. We picked up and dropped off students for families who couldn't afford transportation or take time from work and for those parents who couldn't be bothered with getting their kids to class.

Sometimes we had to turn families away, because there was no more room. I was triumphant and ecstatic! Yes, and I was exhausted! The old me had disappeared. Remember the abused little girl who didn't finish high school? Now I was not only a real-estate millionaire, but also a very successful educationalist and a part time student.

I was riding the crest of a wave and felt elated to have reached the summit of my mountaintop. It had been a long journey. In so many ways I was really fine, provided nobody looked too closely at me, the woman.

5. Loving and Protecting

I had so disappeared into Katie's Kids and its business and human aspects that I did not notice that I still had to continue my personal rebuild. Why should I constantly have to do that? Wasn't I fixed? I was so busy loving and protecting my kids that I had quit paying attention to myself and instead only worried about the company and caring for all the little ones entrusted to me and the staff.

It would be fair to say that I had built a fortress out of the pre-schools to handle the job of protection. The facilities were as advanced as I could make them. They had the highest accreditation possible. I had hired the best teachers and staff based upon the recommendations given to them by the state of Florida. I loved my schools and my kids. They were the beacon in my darkness. They were everything to me, for me, and about me.

My students were not just being babysat or pushed along, only to be left behind. These kids were learning strong educational basics that would carry them well into their scholastic careers. How proud I felt about that. Regardless of what life they were living at home, at Katie's Kids, they knew they were top notch.

Depending upon the school, we could accommodate infants from under one year old to kids up to four years old. The pre-care and aftercare school kids ranged from kindergarteners upward to age thirteen.

The state requirements for infants mandated that there be a teacher for every four students. You're probably laughing at the idea that we regarded our infants as students, but we did. Our teachers were there to stimulate awareness about colors, sounds, shapes, and whatever else was applicable. There was no rap, rock 'n' roll, or Top 40 music played in those rooms, on headphones or otherwise. If my teachers weren't driven to distraction by *Baby Mozart*, the LeapFrog *Letter Factory*, and the like, they had to be deaf! I know the music was imprinted in my brain, because Barbara swore that if I sang "E says 'eh'" one more time, she'd have no choice but to cut out my tongue.

My schools followed the guidelines of the Florida Association for Child Care Management (FACCM) to qualify as an Accredited Professional Pre-school Learning Environment (APPLE). Their protocol for teacher-to-student ratios exceeded those of the state in most areas; the differences were as follows:

	STATE REQUIREMENTS	APPLE REQUIREMENTS
Infants	1 teacher to 4 students	1 teacher to 4 students
Ones	1 teacher to 6 students	1 teacher to 6 students
Twos	1 teacher to 11 students	1 teacher to 8 students
Threes	1 teacher to 15 students	1 teacher to 10 students
Fours	1 teacher to 20 students	1 teacher to 10 students
Aftercare	1 teacher to 25 students	1 teacher to 18 students

Since I had to have those minimums, the staff had to be there, even if my kids called in sick. Consequently, the ratios were at times even better.

My schools provided student meals through the food program provided by Family Central, Inc., a not-for-profit organization dedicated to helping families in need. This allowed each of my children the opportunity to have two square meals on school days (breakfast and lunch), plus a snack time. These meals were catered in and served by the staff.

My staff, too, was very well taken care of. They may have complained back then about whatever they thought Katie's Kids's shortcomings were as an employer, but there is not one of them I have talked to since I closed all the schools that hasn't begged me to start over. They now know how good they really had it.

The staff was overpaid and had good benefits. I was fair about giving them time when their own parental duties called. I knew that the better I took care of my good staff, the better it would be for my kids, and I would also be cared for. I helped many of them personally, sometimes with food and also with their bills and transportation needs. They were treated just like my kids. I wanted everyone in my sphere to be well loved and cared for.

Making everyone happy helped me to thrive in my business venture. I was still struggling on the personal side, and I worked endlessly, often as much as eighteen hours a day, six and seven days a week. My relationship with Barbara was fading faster than it had earlier. When I wasn't working, I was in school either for my commercial driver's license or at Florida Atlantic University, working on my degree.

We had tried to get pregnant and were so disappointed when nothing happened. It seemed we couldn't have kids of our own, and it didn't matter to Barbara or me that we cared for more than three hundred kids who belonged to other people. It wasn't the same.

I could make anyone happy, as long as they were not emotionally attached to me. If an attachment arose, I tended to fail miserably.

I *was* Katie's Kids Learning Center. With over three hundred students, dozens of teachers, staff, and a fleet of vehicles with drivers for student transportation, I could personally travel as much as three hundred miles in a day just keeping up with my chores for our four amazing schools in Palm Beach and Broward Counties.

My schools were Gold Seal- and APPLE-accredited by Florida's Department of Health and FACCM. These superior accreditations took into account a school's accelerated curriculum, staff-to-student ratios, and we went above and beyond the state's standards and requirements for educational excellence. New Delray was on the verge of joining my other schools in receiving the Quality Counts Certificate from the Early Learning Coalition. The ELC had standards for young-educator compliance that were much higher than those set by the state.

My pre-schools were home to me. I remember them all so well. The school in Boynton had a light cream-colored tile throughout the building. There was an airy and open feeling that my dad and I worked hard to create. It had three classrooms: one for two-year-olds, a second for three-year-olds, and a pre-kindergarten classroom for the four-year-olds. There was also an aftercare room next to the administrative office set up for older kids. There was a tiny library in one room with over eight hundred children's books. The resource room held over two hundred teacher resource books and lots of teaching aids, including art materials, science project kits, basic school supplies, and tools for physical education. Hidden away were the Xbox 360 and Wii I had bought for the aftercare kids we had from two thirty to five each afternoon. None of my kids had to pay for any of this. What I didn't get through donations and subsidized funding, I made sure I bought myself.

The Boynton pre-school was located across the street from a park where the aftercare kids could play. The regular students had two enclosed playgrounds on school property. The older kids' playground had a huge slide and a tunnel leading to a smaller slide. There were lot of things to climb on, plus a set of swings. The equipment was decorated in brilliant primary colors. There was even a basketball hoop with its base cemented into the ground.

The younger kids had smaller playground equipment, but it was just as colorful. They had bikes that connected to each other, stationary cars, and picnic tables. We had a commercial easel so the children could draw outside. They also had games, books, and other materials to play with.

The school was on Southeast Second Street in a respectable working-class, residential neighborhood. Many of the forty children we had were of Haitian and Hispanic descent. Some couldn't speak a word of English until we taught it to them. The rest were of African American descent.

Each classroom had the five mandatory center stations. These were designated areas around which children would gather for science, reading, writing, dramatic play, and for housekeeping. All the furniture and materials supplied were of the very best quality.

The walls were painted a light color, with a tree house and a fence woven into the carpeting to give a feeling of playfulness. Some of the classrooms had a sun and a sky with a picket fence on the walls to give the room a friendlier look. Artwork and projects were placed at eye level on a "bragging wall" both children and parents could enjoy. There were red tables with red chairs for all the kids. The red contrasted with the light walls really made that furniture stand out. My Boynton kids had a beautiful place to learn, exercise, and grow.

Down in Broward County, the Margate school was in a white-collar area. This was the only commercial property we owned. Wexford Academy was located at Atlantic Boulevard and Highway 441, directly across the street from Margate Middle School. That location near the middle school meant there were quite a few pre-schools all on the same street, providing plenty of friendly competition for Katie's Kids. The competition didn't affect us. My Margate school was full to capacity with a hundred fifty children, and there was a long waiting list.

About three hundred thousand dollars had gone into rehabbing this pre-school. We replaced walls and light fixtures, built custom cabinetry for the classrooms (and put sinks in them), and updated the bathrooms. We fenced off the huge backyard and made two playgrounds, where we installed spongy flooring instead of the standard mulch.

This school had five huge classrooms. There was a reception area and administrative offices. All the furniture and materials were brand new and top of the line. Floors throughout the school were tiled for easy cleanup. There was a large resource room that held our library. This space boasted over three thousand children's books and hundreds of educational resource books for the teachers. That's where we stored all the science class kits, arts and crafts materials, and all the standard school supplies that we provided free to the children. Each classroom had the five centers for activities covering the areas of science, reading, writing, playtime, and housekeeping.

There were no infants at Wexford. The younger children, the one- and two-year-olds, had their own wing. Their rooms had doors to the outside. This made it easier for them to reach their playground. They had the stationary commercial cars to sit in, bikes, several miniature picnic tables, a playhouse, and Little Tikes slides. There was an outdoor art center with easels and plenty of toys.

The older children had picnic tables also, but theirs were adult sized. They had bikes, other riding toys, and a playhouse. There was an outdoor art center for them too, as well as games, books, and other materials for them to play with. Their large playground had one side devoted to rock climbing, and there were two slides and tons of things to climb upon. There was a permanent basketball hoop and a large, separate mulched area where the kids could play field sports.

The entire facility and the grounds were protected by cameras and a computerized security platform. The director of Wexford could watch everything going on anywhere at the school in real time. I would have liked to have had at least three more large pre-schools along the lines of what we had at Wexford.

Old Delray was situated on Northeast Third Avenue in a residential neighborhood. We only had three- and four-year-olds at Old Delray. There were forty-seven who came to school every day for education, exercise, and meals.

Here also we used light-colored tile throughout the building. This school had a truly open and airy atmosphere, because the classroom areas had been turned into one enormous room. We divided the space up into three separate areas with furniture designed for the purpose.

This totally open layout meant that the teachers at Old Delray had to be on their toes to maintain proper student behavior. At times, that was a real struggle for them. I always appreciated their efforts so much. These teachers were dealing with some very difficult kids.

As always, I provided a separate resource room that held hundreds of teacher resource books and a wealth of learning materials for art, and of course there were science project kits, basic school supplies, and physical education tools.

At this school, there was only one quite large community area for all the children to play in. Playtimes were organized by age group. Similar to the playgrounds at the other schools, this one had huge slides and plenty of fun things to climb on, and a basketball hoop was cemented into the ground.

I was on a financial roll and exceeding personal bests in happiness as the calendar headed into 2009. Despite the economic collapse from which so many were suffering, I was monetarily sound. I found that money could buy lots of things: the undivided attention of children, loyal employees, and all kinds of new friends. Of course, I didn't notice (or perhaps I ignored) that just about everyone had a hand out, happy to accept my largesse; some had good reason, while others had their own agendas. By the time I was considering the next school, I felt more at peace than ever. I had come a long way from those miserable times in Massachusetts.

The last school to open was New Delray. It was on Tenth Avenue, which was a very poor neighborhood just a few blocks from the sophisticated and pricy shops and restaurants of Atlantic Avenue. What a contrast between The Avenue and my school less than a mile away. On Atlantic, you could valet park your car and spend two hundred dollars on a dinner for two. Despite its proximity to the playground of the wealthy, I was nevertheless scared to leave New Delray alone at night. There were drug dealers on the street corners. These nefarious dudes would pretend to be selling tee shirts at two in the morning. Now there's a brilliant disguise.

When I took possession, the condition of this school was the worst I had encountered; it was the one where we had to bring in the construction crew to redo the whole place before we could open it to the needy children of the area. There were two buildings on the property, with a large backyard and a big, concrete parking lot in front.

There was already fencing around the property's backyard, but it was chain-link and in horrible condition. We tore it all down and replaced it with six-foot-tall privacy fencing. This way, the children could escape from the reality of the neighborhood and feel that they were in a safe and loving environment. We split the yard into two playgrounds.

The older kids had their own playground with a slide and other big equipment. It was painted in brilliant colors and had lots of places to climb and run. The playground for the smaller kids had Little Tikes equipment along with a commercial-grade swing set featuring safety-minded seats in different styles specifically designed for toddlers and for infants. Again, there were connected bikes for them to ride and the requisite age-appropriate picnic tables. They had our preferred outdoor art center, just as at the other schools, and those poor kids had all the toys they could want. We made that property beautiful.

New Delray had a huge capacity for infants. That's why I had laminate wood flooring installed throughout the common areas and classrooms. While tile would have cost less, I didn't want to see an infant fall down on such a hard floor. The walls were painted a light, warm color that encouraged children to feel happy and calm.

Between the two buildings, we had seventy-eight young charges in our care spread between five classrooms. The infants and one-year-olds shared a building with the administrative offices and resource storage. The two-, three-, and four-year-olds shared the other building with the aftercare kids.

Each Katie's Kids Learning Center provided structured physical education activities. We believed that a healthy body supports a strong mind, and vice versa. We served two nutritious meals every day and provided a snack break. It's much easier to learn when your body is well fed. Many of our kids did not have that luxury at home.

By the end of 2009, I had four full-capacity pre-schools teeming with hundreds of kids. I loved every building and each kid with my whole being. I truly felt that with the educational groundwork being laid, the free food programs, the after-hours care, and all the personal interventions I had with families, I was protecting my kids from their hard everyday lives while preparing them for the big, bad future.

I expected similar dedication from all my dozens of staff members. Hiring teachers, teacher's aides, and bus drivers was a very complicated and exacting business. It's so important to pick candidates who really want to work with children in large groups. Some people just don't have that kind of personality. We required highly qualified people to work with our children.

Criminal background checks were necessary for validating an applicant's credentials. We began by contacting the appropriate local law-enforcement authorities, and every employee application must also be referred to the state. Applicants must submit fingerprints, and the state then performs a background check. For those with clean backgrounds, the state issues a letter of approval. To my mind, though, the state has strange ideas about what sort of criminal histories do or do not disqualify a candidate from suitability, but who questions Florida — or any state? On top of all that, Tallahassee was incredibly backlogged on background checks all the time.

In my opinion, the state of Florida ought to take another look at what type of criminal history should bar someone from working with children. There should be a proper threshold or dividing line somewhere that disqualifies an applicant, or, on the other hand, that allows someone to be approved despite a criminal record.

Most of the time, a person with a good personality who fit our requirements was hired on a probationary basis until all the approvals could be reported. We especially considered those recommended by a current employee.

The group of staff I had at the beginning of 2010 worked like a well-oiled machine. There were plenty of office politics and clashes of personality, but we were doing stressful work for lots of little people with huge attitudes. My staff worked hard for their money and I paid them well.

Not all of the children were bright and shining examples of angelic childhood. Wouldn't it be boring if they were all perfect? Some were very quiet and shy, some were extremely outgoing and friendly, and some were just tiny terrorists.

We usually could forgive a child by understanding the type of upbringing he or she was receiving and the harsh environment where he or she was being raised. It was rare that we kicked anybody out. Everything usually worked out. Then there came the kid who was in and out in five days.

This child could make Dante's *Inferno* seem like a trip to Disneyland. If something wasn't tied down, he'd steal it. If it wasn't broken, he'd break it. If it was clean, he'd find a way to muss it up. He was cantankerous and would bite, scratch, and punch anything that didn't run faster than he could. This was all before the tender age of five. I understood real fast why the director and teacher couldn't find out from the boy's mom where he'd been in pre-school before. She wasn't dumb enough to tell us.

This rascal of a boy was in the Voluntary Prekindergarten (VPK) program at Katie's Kids in Boynton, and he had the entire place in an uproar. Everyone was so in shock over his destructiveness that it took a couple of days for anyone to react. On his fifth day, the whole school had a field trip to a park. Being a conscientious owner and knowing the personality of the majority of my kids, I always sent extra staff to protect the general public when we travelled en masse. I had two extra adults for the trip, but to say the day was complete chaos would be lying. It was a fucking nightmare. I can say that because I'm an adult, and I was there. And it describes the day perfectly.

This kid — we'll call him Dante — tripped a teacher on purpose and laughed when she fell, and broke a limb off a small ornamental tree and began pummeling the other kids with it. He whipped out his penis and peed all over the slide, and as if that weren't bad enough, he was dry humping toddlers like some rabid dog. Four of us, me and three teachers, had such a time trying to wrestle him between us so we could grab him without injuring him or hurting ourselves. Remember that this is the school with a capacity of forty little souls! If you think the rest of those little pranksters didn't take full advantage of the situation, you'd be wrong, very wrong! Four supervising adults distracted by one brat left something like nineteen of them unsupervised. It was anarchy at its best. By the time we were finished for the day, not one amongst them had a manner left!

It's actually quite hilarious to think back on it now, but at the time, all I could envision was my being arrested for public disgrace or something. It took all four of us to carry little Dante back to the bus, each of us taking a hand or foot. That way, nobody got hurt. By the time we got back to school, that little turd had single-handedly changed my moral stance on corporal punishment. There would not have been a paddle big enough for him or an adjective all-encompassing enough to describe the joy I'd have felt hitting him with it.

The look on his mother's face when I handed over her child for the last time was payback enough. She chewed me up one side and down the other about leaving her in the lurch. Then she turned on him. I do not think she had ever told him no before, but he soon got the message. It does a body good to see justice done. To see the look on his face when she went after him was priceless.

I'd have loved to see a mixed-martial-arts, no-holds-barred match between ol' Dante and a boy I'll call Whitey. Now, don't get your panties in a knot. I am the least bigoted person I know. I'm part white myself and extremely mature, and besides, he started it. This kid would set the civil rights movement back five decades if he had known what it was. His bloodline was from Alabama. He was in the care of foster parents who seemed sweet enough, and they felt compelled to explain the background. He was as white as the driven snow, blond, and blue eyed. (I had always envisioned the devil as dark haired for some reason...you know what I mean?)

Whitey was all of about thirty inches tall, nearly five years old, and his favorite word was "nigger." His second favorite was "spic." Now, I will not disparage his intelligence or anything, and I give him credit for being brave, but nonetheless, when you are tiny and in the true minority in close quarters, you might want to watch your mouth. I'm just saying that that'd be the prudent thing.

He attended pre-school in a place where the population of students was around 30 percent African American, 40 percent Haitian, 29 percent Hispanic, and then there was ol' Whitey. About the only other Caucasians were staff, and they were few.

The staff would constantly try to redirect his terminology, because they couldn't really tell him no or call him racist. They tried bribing him, but nothing worked. Conferences with the foster parents were a waste of time, for them and for us, because he would not listen, and they were at their wits' end. There's no way the state could have helped. You'd have been able to hear them laughing all the way to wherever you live if I called them about a kid with a bad vocabulary.

One fine day, a teacher of the four-year-olds was engaged in cleaning up the art center out on the playground, and the teacher's aide was tending a booboo, when our little friend used one or more of his favorite words one too many times and far enough away from the teachers that they couldn't react. We don't know which words they were exactly, because he *refuses to ever say them again*! Let's just say his classmates had had enough, and they went vigilante. It took about one minute. That kid had two black eyes, his shirt was ripped, his nose was bloodied, and he had a split lip. You should have seen the poor little kid. Humph!

We filled out the appropriate paperwork for such an incident, and the foster parents didn't choose to pursue further action. Over his head they just smiled at each other as they took him for the rest of the day. Justice may sometimes indeed be blind. Nobody said it couldn't come wrapped in tiny packages.

Don't get me wrong, I loved those two troubled kids as much as I did all the others. You can't discriminate. My kids were up against bad odds. Most of them came to us from poor families and tough streets. They aged extremely fast. They got along as best they could, frankly, until somebody knocked some sense into them. If this happened at such a young age, it would hopefully deter them from provoking someone later in life who'd just as soon pull a gun as give them a bloody nose. It happens out there more than you or I want to know.

By the end of the 2009 through the 2010 school year, I had arrived at the summit of happiness. I had climbed the mountain of pain I'd been toiling up most of my life, and I had kicked the rocks off the top. This was living!

I was extremely successful. I was educating, loving, and protecting children who I felt needed it the most, and I was content. My seven-year journey in young-child care had so many blessings. I had students I had taught come to visit me as they entered middle school to thank me for the grounded beginnings I'd given them. I had aftercare kids who were preparing for college and were never too cool to say hello to Ms. Katie and give her a hug and kiss if we met by chance.

My past had faded into nothingness. I was Katie's Kids.

6. A Tainted Vacation

By the spring of 2010, though, I needed a break. I had been working sixteen hours a day, six and seven days a week, for years now. I'd never been able to take much time off. Barbara and a friend thought the time had come and that the three of us should go on a vacation somewhere together. Could I do it? It was so hard to be away from the schools. I weighed the options. I had not had an extended break for years. A few days here and there didn't amount to much. The idea was very, very appealing to me — besides which, Barbara and I needed some time away together to recoup and see where we were.

I gathered the troops, meaning all the teachers and directors, my caring staff, and asked them if they thought they could handle the pre-schools if I went away on a long vacation. There was a huge, collective sigh, and they agreed unanimously that they could. I had become so tough on them that by now they had given me an alter ego named "Kevin" that they would use to disparage me in my presence without being insubordinate. They invoked Kevin quite often and threatened frequently to burn him in effigy! My trusted staff assured me that everything would be fine and not to worry.

With that reassurance, I decided to go. I owed Barbara that much. We'd been together almost a decade and a half, and outside of my dad's family vacations, we'd not spent much time together alone. The short holidays with Dad's family weren't always a success, either. I didn't communicate with them much anymore, and it is hard to travel with people who think they know you but don't. And poor Barbara didn't know them at all. Nobody judged; it was just tough without much communication.

It was time for Barbara and me to reconnect, because everything had become about the pre-schools. I would answer business calls while out at dinner. Sometimes calls came in as late as midnight, and the phone would start ringing again bright and early at five in the morning.

This was the life we lived. I worked somewhere between ninety and one hundred hours a week. We would go shopping for personal things and end up on business errands. I couldn't help it. I was consumed by the pre-schools. They were everything.

Barbara's birthday and our anniversary are on the same day. One year I forgot, like so much in my life that was personal. Private things took a backseat to the pre-schools. The day I forgot, Barbara had been shoveling mulch with me for hours at one of the pre-schools when, all of a sudden, I noticed she was in tears. She was crying because I had never wished her a happy birthday or a happy anniversary. I forgot! How could I? Am I a complete asshole? I couldn't help it. I felt so sad and sorry. Here I was, trying to be perfect professionally, and screwing up the most personal relationship of all, the relationship with my partner. I had a lot to learn about personal relationships.

When we were preparing to leave for Europe, I was extremely anxious about leaving all my babies and the responsibility for the business to my staff. Perhaps I was having a premonition, because I became hesitant. As a backup plan, I even told the pre-school consultant, to whom I had been paying profound amounts of money for about six years, to check up on everyone and answer any questions the staff might have while I was away. She told me it wouldn't be a problem. She knew my schools almost as well as I. I just had more invested in them.

By the beginning of July 2010, I had a total of five directors and the consultant to look after the shop. Each had between ten and twenty years or more of experience in the pre-school sector, collectively more than eighty years of continuous, hands-on training. I decided my lifeblood was in qualified hands and that I could go on the trip to relax and have a little fun. I wanted to break the mold of the past several years. I didn't like that I had become a complete workaholic. I needed to change and not be so focused upon the pre-schools and the business that surrounded them. I wanted time for me. I needed time off. It wasn't too much to ask, was it?

Where do I begin? Certainly it's a vacation I will never forget, not ever! Not only because it was a long, trying, and enlightening trip, but more because the absence from Katie's Kids inevitably brought so much pain. It was a vacation like no other. To put it succinctly, we did home-exchange programs, stayed at a couple of hostels, and did couch surfing. It took me out of my comfort zone. My OCD personality couldn't define a zone this bad. We were doing the vacation on such a tight budget that you'd have thought we were strapped for cash! Money should have been the last of our concerns.

Barbara had been going on trips with her best friend Abbé for years. Barbara had always complained that I just didn't want to vacation with her. It's true, I didn't—most especially because of the way she and Abbé traveled. Maybe in this one respect I had been spoiled a bit. I was used to going on vacation with my grandmother, who always stayed at five-star hotels, traveled in limousines, and took cruises in suites. Who cared about soaking up the local ambiance and mixing with the masses? Grandma could see it just fine driving by.

When we got to Copenhagen, I was apprehensive. I was on edge because we were going to be staying in a house that wasn't ours. What if someone came home, forgot we were there, came into the house, and killed us for trespassing? I managed to deal with it and stayed anyway, but I didn't get much sleep.

Once we were getting settled into this Danish house, I e-mailed the staff direct to their telephones. I needed to know how everything was going and asked that they write back immediately. The return e-mails arrived soon after, saying "Everything is fine, Katie, just as we told you." *Everything will be fine, don't worry, go and have some fun and relax.* Barbara told me that they had also reassured her by e-mail, writing that everything would be all right and to take it easy.

What is relaxation, anyway? My phone wasn't ringing every five minutes. I had no one yelling my name. No directors were calling me at the last minute to do a bus run because the CDL driver didn't show up. I wasn't cleaning around toilets where twenty-five little boys were not hitting the mark. I wasn't squeezed behind a toxic-smelling dumpster because the staff was too lazy to make sure that the garbage they threw at it actually went in and not over! I wasn't holding a crying child who'd suffered a bruise or little cut. I wasn't talking to a parent. I had no fires to put out. I had complete silence for what seemed like the first time in seven years. How was I supposed to deal with this? It was making me bat-shit crazy! Who the hell can relax when you don't know what's going on? It was just Barbara, Abbé, me, and nothing else. I was lost. I had no schedule.

The first couple of days were really hard, but each day did get a little easier. I would sneak to the computer though, every hour on the hour, to see how the pre-schools were doing. The only time I didn't stress was on the weekend. The pre-schools were closed; we no longer had weekend hours. One day, Abbé decided she wanted to go exploring. Barbara went with her, but I stayed behind. At this point I was just happy to do nothing. I was enjoying the moment, and surprise of all surprises, I was reading a book a day, or almost a full book a day. I never read much because of ADHD, and I thought I still hated reading, but here I was in Copenhagen, reading a book in a stranger's house! I was relaxed, and I was enjoying it.

The next day, the neighbors came over to offer us a traditional Danish lunch. It was one that they would normally send along with their children to take to school. Now, there was something to get excited about—school and food. I was up for anything—until I saw the plates arrive at the dining table. Apprehensive doesn't begin to describe how I felt. I'm a very finicky eater. I have no idea what they served us. The presentation looked so beautiful, but to my eyes, the food was quite unappetizing. It was in five pieces, neatly spread out. All I know is that one was a piece of raw fish stacked onto something else. This was not sushi. The smell made me gag, but I needed to be polite and had to talk myself through it. I told myself that I was a fully grown woman and I could do it. That's when I took the most disgusting-looking piece off the plate and swallowed it whole. That was followed by warm Diet Pepsi, which in itself was gross, but I drank the whole thing so I couldn't taste what I'd taken off the plate. Yes! I had done it! Then I ground my teeth and moved on to the next piece, all the while praying they had a six-pack of Diet Pepsi for me.

As I managed to choke down another piece, I looked around at my lunch mates. Everyone was scarfing the food down as if there were no tomorrow. My eyes grew round with amazement. How could they eat with such relish? I needed to get through this meal without disgracing myself, by — God forbid — heaving the whole lot back up onto my plate! I never asked what we were eating that day. I didn't want to know, and I never wanted to see or smell anything like it again.

I needed more to drink and asked our hostess if I might have another Diet Pepsi. She explained that American soft drinks were something quite special and that they rarely drank them and how sorry she was that they had no more to offer. I knew then that I would really prefer to be back in the good old USA, the junk food capital of the world. We had been in Europe less than a week, and there were four weeks more to go. Heaven help me.

Abbé decided that we should head to Germany next to visit Barbara's home-exchange friend from high school. I was OK with that, since I really just wanted to relax and check on the pre-schools every hour, on the hour.

We stopped in Hamburg, where we stayed at a youth hostel. I had never been to one; this was a new experience for me. They explained that most people who stay in a hostel are under thirty years old, and we were pushing it. That was good for me to hear, and I suggested we go to a hotel instead. Barbara gave me the evil eye. I shut the hell up. Then it was explained that you have to share a room with other people. That didn't appeal to me at all. I thought, *You've got to be kidding. We have to share a room with strangers?* It got worse for me when we were told that this included the possibility of sharing a room with guys! I almost passed out, because I don't do guys in any way, shape, or form, and I definitely was not interested in having a stranger who was a guy in the bed next to mine, even if we were in Hamburg, Germany! I slouched onto a chair and buried my head in my hands. What had I gotten myself into?

We walked up the stairs to our room. It wasn't bad at all, and it was very clean. It would have been OK if it weren't for the fact that we could have another guest. Abbé and Barbara opened the door with such excitement, while all I could think about was wondering what the hell they had gotten me into this time. I'd seen the movie *Hostel*. It's a bloody, terrifying story that traumatized me for months.

I sat on one of the twin beds, my hands holding my head up. I stared at the wall for about fifteen minutes until Abbé told me everything was going to work out fine. I put a half grin on my face and wrestled myself out of the panic attack that had been brewing. I chanted to myself about one of the main purposes of this European vacation. It was supposed to bring Barbara and me closer together. With that thought in mind, I repeatedly told myself, *Kathryn, it is OK. Like Abbé said, everything will be all right; everything's going to be OK.*

That's when the door to our room flew open. Standing there was a young woman in her mid-twenties who was upset because she thought she was going to be in a room with immature teens. Man, was she ever happy to see us. I didn't realize it immediately, but boy, was I happy to see her too. She'd tipped the scale of occupancy, and we probably wouldn't get a guy. Whew!

She told us a little bit about herself. She stayed at this hostel Monday through Friday because where she lived, she couldn't find a job. After speaking on that subject for a little while, her boyfriend called her. I had never heard of Skype before. She started to talk to her boyfriend and was kissing the screen when

Barbara and Abbé ushered me out of the room to go downstairs. I am totally handicapped when it comes to social cues. I would've stayed and watched and listened. Out of courtesy, Barbara and Abbé took me downstairs where they began to plan our itinerary for the following day.

This was my chance to e-mail the staff. I didn't want to be a party pooper, but I did want to make sure all was well at the schools and with all my children and staff. The text reply that came back told me to stop bothering them! Oh! That was good. I thought I could get my head back into being on vacation. No one noticed that I'd run off to send and receive e-mails, as I wasn't gone for too long. Barbara smiled at me when I got back. She was so delighted to have my whole, undivided attention centered on her. Everything was good in relationship land.

You would've had to see the low-budget car those two scrooges rented to believe it. I was wedged into the area laughingly called the backseat. My left leg was straddling a pile of luggage, and I'm pretty sure my other one got lodged somewhere up my right nostril whenever we hit a bump. I had to just sleep, because my arms were so squished against my boobs I could hardly breathe, much less read.

After being in the car for what seemed like days, we arrived at the home of Barbara's old friend. Finally, I met Kristen and her family. They were so very nice to us. Thank God, they spoke English. Of course, the children didn't, but at least I could communicate with the adults. Besides, all children speak the language of love with their smiles, hugs, and kisses. Abbé decided she would take the middle-floor bedroom, while Barbara and I took one in the basement. I thought we were getting the crappy end of the stick until Abbé told us that Kristen's daughter got up at seven every morning, whined piercingly in German, and stomped her feet loudly when she walked on the bare floor above. Now I was thankful for the basement and being left undisturbed. At this point, I didn't want to listen to any child whine, even if he or she were mine! I was having a peaceful vacation away from my three hundred south Florida whiners.

One day, Kristen planned something special for us. They took us to a shooting festival. It was unlike anything we have in the United States. It's all about who is going to be king. The men who want to be king have to spend a lot of money for a chance at the crown. More to the point, they have to be accurate shots as they take aim at a bird that is hung way up in the sky. (Don't be alarmed, the bird is already dead.) The man who shoots the bird loose from its tether and causes it to fall to the earth becomes king. I couldn't even see what was holding the bird up there, it was so distant, much less be able to take aim, fire, and hit the thing. I had never seen shooting like this before. It was as if we'd been transported back in time to watch Robin Hood split the arrow and win a kiss from Maid Marian. I enjoyed the festival immensely, and the park grounds were stunning. I found it curious that this park was open for just one day every year, just for the shooting festival.

Bread is a staple of the German diet. German people love their bread, and on shooting festival day I had more than my share, celebrating to the point where I would have to consider shooting myself if I had another piece. We genuinely enjoyed our time with Kristen and her family, but we ate too much bread! I thought the three of us would turn into dinner rolls!

From Kristen's we were off again, heading north to return to Scandinavia. We travelled through Norway and Sweden and a couple of other places I don't quite remember, since I was still squished in one of our little European rental cars. All I remember is that we had so much fun laughing and sharing new experiences together. I was enjoying being with Barbara and away from the toils at home. I also was feeling a newfound sense of solitude and was able to relax. At least, I think I was relaxing.

If there was e-mail available, I would send messages hour after hour, and sometimes, in more neurotic moments, I would telephone—a lot. I can hear the school staff saying, "Oh, no, it's Kevin again; Kevin's driving us crazy!" And here I thought I was being laid back about things. Don't you just love loyalty?

The last day of our vacation, I sent so many texts to my trusted team. Back in Florida, everyone was so excited I'd soon be home and each was trying to figure out how to corner me once I was back to ask to be the next to take a vacation. They were all happy that everything had gone well for us in Europe, but most of all they were thrilled that I was just hours away from returning to run Katie's Kids. The staff had done fine all the time we were away. They told me to please not text them anymore and for me to just relax because they'd see me soon.

I thought about what they said, and for once, I listened. The next day as we prepared to fly out of Denmark, I didn't text them once. I was happy they had held the pre-schools together. After we boarded the plane, I went directly to sleep. Later on, when I woke I found myself so anxious. I wanted to get back to work and into the swing of things. I remember talking to another business owner on the plane about getting back to work. We both were excited to be returning to the United States and our companies.

When we finally got to New York after our transatlantic flight, we learned that our next flight back to West Palm Beach had been cancelled. We thought that maybe we could fly into the Fort Lauderdale or the Miami airports. There were no flights available going to south Florida. I remember being so bummed about that, because I desperately wanted to get home to my family. By "family," I mean the children and the staff. I had been gone five weeks, and I was craving me some Katie's Kids! I had told Abbé that we had better let Helen, my friend and a seasonal teacher at Katie's Kids, know the flight was cancelled so she wouldn't be waiting at the airport for us. Abbé called while I piled up the luggage on one of those wheeled carts. When I turned back to her, I noticed her facial expression had changed drastically. She was green. I thought she was going to be sick all over the luggage carousel. I was absolutely shocked, because nothing bothered Abbé, not even that horrendous food in Copenhagen.

What could possibly be wrong? I asked myself. I couldn't figure it out. Abbé whispered something for a couple more seconds — it seemed an eternity — and handed the phone over. I asked her what was wrong. She turned away and she gave me no answer. "What's wrong?" I cried. She told me she didn't want to be the one to tell me.

Oh my God, what is wrong? Please God, nothing awful! I looked at that phone like it was a coiled snake ready to strike. I didn't want to touch it. Then, for a second, I thought, I *know it can't be about the pre-schools. I just talked to everyone yesterday from Denmark.* So I took the phone from her.

At first, all I heard was silence. Then a calm voice asked if I had heard what had happened. "What do you mean, what happened?" I gasped back at her. I didn't know anything, and at that moment wished I didn't need to know. I stared at the slowly moving carousel as if in a trance. Something very bad was coming.

In a low tone, she told me — these are Helen's words — "Katie, today a child died because she was left in a van for six hours at one of your facilities."

I thought, *How could that be possible?* I couldn't have heard her right. I wanted to scream, "Can you repeat that?" But instead, I blacked out and crashed onto the terminal floor. Cracking my head on the carousel edge jolted me back to consciousness as I questioned if I had really heard what Helen had said. There I was, lying on the floor with the phone talking somewhere in my hand, I think, but where was my hand? I was discombobulated, and felt like I would be sick. I couldn't be sick, because what I needed was for Helen to unsay those words that a child at one of my facilities had died after being left in one of my vehicles. She needed to take those words back.

Grief and pain set in, and I wondered if all this was really happening. Maybe I was in a bad dream and couldn't break out to consciousness. I kept telling myself to wake up, wake up! The ceiling seemed to sway, and the floor was spinning. I lay there curled up and keening, wanting to be put out of my misery like a wounded animal whose humane end is immediate death.

Abbé at that point took the phone from me. I lay there on that dirty carpet in the middle of the baggage claim in one of the largest airports in America, rocking back and forth. I kept thinking this couldn't be. After all, just before leaving on vacation, I had held a two-hour meeting with staff about van safety. I was very particular about transportation safety. It was one of the things I had spent so much time on. It was my rule: my kids must always be protected. Period! How the hell did this happen with all the checks and balances in my schools? In a pre-school, if someone makes a mistake, things are organized so that someone else should catch it. When a driver signs off on delivery of the kids, the director physically checks the vehicles to see that everyone is accounted for and signs off on the arrivals. This could not happen in my school. I couldn't believe it.

By now, many people had noticed my odd behavior, and someone called security. Abbé and Barbara explained the situation to them and they helped pick me up off the floor, bundled me into a wheelchair, and took me somewhere private and quiet. I don't recall exactly where they took me or what they said or how anybody else was taking the news. I was in a torture zone no one should ever have to enter, and I didn't know if I'd get out. I'm still not sure that I have. I just learned to hide it better.

Once I regained my composure, I started calling the staff directors to see what was going on. First, I wanted to make sure everyone else was OK, and then I wanted to know how this had happened. I just couldn't believe this was my reality. I wanted to know if the parents had been contacted, and I wanted to know the name of the child. I finally got hold of one of the directors, who told me she couldn't talk to me because she was dealing with police officers. She hung up on me. I was furious. How could she just hang up?

I waited a few minutes and called again. No answer. I was dying inside. I was stuck in New York and couldn't do anything, no matter how much I wanted to. I was plain helpless. I paced the room like a caged tiger. I bounced on my toes, ready to run, to bolt to anywhere but where I was. I kept praying that someone would pick up a phone when I called. I wanted to know what was going on. I was a screaming, frantic mess. I wanted to make sure the other children were OK and that they were being taken safely to their homes. There were still no answers. I started hyperventilating, because I wasn't there, and they were shutting me out. I was tearing at my hair and darting ferocious looks at everyone in sight. I was scaring the hell out of Barbara and Abbé.

By now, the airport security personnel were convinced I was loony tunes, and once they'd zeroed in on my name, they were seriously spooked. They had a crazed, black, Muslim woman on their hands, and I could tell they were itching to frisk me just to be sure I wasn't wired to blow. I was done with sitting around, with everyone afraid to look at me.

I stomped out of the airport with Barbara and Abbé in tow to make sure I could get phone reception just in case anyone called me back. I got another director on the line, and she said she couldn't talk at all. When the head director finally picked up her phone, she said she couldn't talk long. She told me there was a mob outside of the pre-school and that the police were afraid for the safety of the children and the staff. The police and the staff were moving the remaining students to a church down the street, where the parents would be able to pick up their children.

I was helpless and didn't know what to do. I wanted to do something, anything. I was so consumed by what was happening, I hadn't realized how much time had passed. We'd been at the airport for hours.

The girls insisted we go to a hotel and get a room, but I wanted to stay at the airport just in case a magical flight appeared. Something, anything, was better than being stuck here.

I couldn't keep a linear thought in my head except for *Please God, help me, what did I do wrong? Please God, please God*, and *Let this be a bad dream.* Even though I knew my friends were right about not getting a flight out, I still wished and prayed. They finally got me into a taxicab by threatening to leave me alone at the airport. I felt like I had been drinking all day. I hadn't, of course. I was just ridden with guilt that I hadn't been there for that child. I just couldn't think of anything but that poor baby, and the directors weren't calling. *Please call! Please call me!*

I stayed up all night trying to reach the staff. I had to know that everyone else was safe. Through the dark night, I spoke to each of my directors, dragging them all out of tortured sleeps. I especially remember talking to Petra Rodriguez, the director at New Delray. One of her responsibilities was to check the van as the second signature, ensuring that all children were off the bus.

At first I couldn't get her to talk. Petra just cried and cried. Once she got herself together and could talk, she apologized. She said she couldn't believe this was happening; she had been in childcare for over twenty years and nothing like this had ever happened to anybody she knew. Through her tears, she told me the health department had said we needed to close the pre-school the following day.

I didn't know for sure if this was true, because I had not heard from the attorney for the health department. I didn't have her number, and she hadn't contacted me, so I told everyone to open the next day unless I told them otherwise. I didn't want the parents who had to work to lose their jobs.

The next day, all the pre-schools were open, and I received a call from Petra saying the health department attorney wanted to speak with me. I told Petra to make sure to give her my number. The attorney called and asked me if I would close down voluntarily while they completed their investigation and said that if I didn't, they would close me down anyway. I told the staff to listen to the health department and to close the school. The attorney asked me to stop transporting children from and to their homes at the other pre-schools until the investigation was finished. I agreed to these terms also. I didn't know what else to do. This was going to be a colossal nightmare for those parents who relied upon our transportation. I needed to conform to the attorney's dictates. An innocent baby had died. Ultimately, I was responsible.

I sat in that New York hotel room in the waning night and needed to cry for the loss of that baby and the destruction of my little empire. But I didn't cry. I had not known how to express my emotions from the time I was twelve years old when Butch started messing with me. I would not give him the satisfaction of knowing he was hurting me, so I made myself immune to crying. Now that I needed that most basic outlet, I didn't have it. All the emotions building up inside me were not going to have a way out. My world as I knew it was falling apart around me, and I was becoming a ticking time bomb. I knew nothing would ever be the same.

7. Innocence Lost

While I was stuck in New York, reeling emotionally and psychologically and in the demented pursuit of a flight home, my family in Florida was shattered.

There was not one child in any of the schools who didn't hear about the death of Haile Brockington. It was front-page news and headlined on radio and television. The loss of little Haile could not help but have an impact on them. Their well-ordered lives at Katie's Kids essentially crumbled. The parents of all the children who used our transport were naturally quite traumatized by Haile's death. At the same time, and with very little notice, they had to figure out how to get their kids to and from school. Some had to drive a great distance out of their way, since New Delray was shut because of the investigation. Each child was accommodated somewhere temporarily at another of our other locations or was harbored in a neighboring pre-school. The staff sheltered the kids as best they could, but the vultures known as news reporters had no shame and questioned a child if they had the opportunity and thought they could get away with it. Some news-people even shoved microphones through the school's playground fences until they got busted and were told to stop by police. We were thankful for that.

There were missteps, too. The police, on the day of the incident and obviously without thinking of the effect their words might have, actually told some of the two-year-olds that Haile was dead. Some of the parents of these little ones were incensed that their children had been told so bluntly. What a horrific mess. Those darling innocents didn't need to be exposed to the loss of their friend so insensitively. It was bad enough having the coroner's van out front all afternoon and the entire school yard draped in bold crime-scene tape marking the place where Haile had died. Strangers were crawling through every square inch of the school, looking grim and terrifying. We won't even discuss how reprehensible the neighbors were, mobbing the school and throwing rocks at the staff as they tried to talk to police and later, when they were removing the children. The students were sad and understandably confused. What the hell were our neighbors thinking? That the staff had planned this nightmare?

Every member of my staff felt annihilated. They were generally very good people who had given their lives to the care of children. They chose to work in that troubled neighborhood and with its many difficult kids. They loved their jobs and went about them tirelessly, exceeding all expectations. Because of a horrible dereliction of duty by a few, the others were thrust out of innocent servitude into a realm of guilt no one should be forced to endure. They now resided in the psychologically torturous world of "what-ifs."

Every adult at New Delray was a suspect by association. Each was grilled by police and disparaged by the neighbors. They were all hounded to their homes by news crews. They tore themselves up wondering, *What if I'd done this or what if I'd done that*? That day was so devastating that many found they had to leave their careers in child care.

Patricia Daniels was an assistant teacher at New Delray. Hers was the classroom for the two-year-olds where Haile spent her days. Her own child, N'gozi-Herce TikurLib, was Haile's classmate. Patricia is a loving mother of six children, many of whom graduated from Katie's Kids Learning Center. She believed in powerful names for her children. She expected important things from her offspring. Patricia started working for me in December of 2009 and started as a driver. She became an assistant teacher through her intelligence and desire to be more instrumental in childhood development. She was trained in infant CPR and first aid and was earning her state Child Development Associate (CDA) certification, which I required of all my assistant teachers (it's a comprehensive course provided by the state that certifies early-childhood teachers.)

I loved having Patricia on my staff because of all the real-life, at-home training she'd had with her own family. That's one reason why we let her take on the two-year-old classroom. She was crazy enough to ask for it when most people run from two-year-olds, but she also wanted to oversee N'gozi's very specific diet.

On August 5, 2010, she had been relegated temporarily to the infant classroom because Petra Rodriguez, the director of New Delray, wanted her elsewhere and intended to prepare the two-year-old classroom for my return. Patricia was confused by the move but did as she was told. The two-year-olds' teacher, Michelle, had been given a mandatory unscheduled vacation day. Petra felt she was personally the only one who could clean and prep the room correctly to meet my high standards. So the stage was set for disaster: neither of the permanent staff assigned to the classroom were in it that day.

Petra Rodriguez was the director of New Delray, with over twenty years of experience in early childhood education. She had her own way of doing things based upon that experience and was of the type who believed that she always knew best. All the classrooms in all the schools were subject to my high standards of cleanliness and structure, and she believed that Michelle and Patricia were lax in the maintenance of theirs. This was quite unfair of her, because anyone with a two-year-old knows they can be less predictable and more destructive than a Category 5 hurricane. People don't call that age "the terrible twos" for nothing! Michelle and Patricia dealt with a whole gaggle of these kids daily. What was the possibility of keeping the room absolutely perfect at all times?

That day, the children were all picked up at their homes and brought to school by Amanda Inman, a new driver who had been hired while I was away with Barbara and Abbé. An employee at one of our other schools personally vouched for Amanda after she was recommended to come and work with us by the Work Force Alliance. I had maintained close contact with my staff while away and was aware that Amanda was driving for us. With personal and professional recommendations, what reason would I have had to be worried about her qualifications and suitability to the responsible position of driving children to and from their pre-school? The staff assured me she was doing fine and that the state would have notified us if she was unsuitable, right?

Patricia told me that she had offered to train Amanda on the transport together with the route, since she herself had been driving it earlier in the year. She also said she would explain the sign-off procedures. But Petra told her that it was unnecessary for Patricia to be involved and that she'd handle everything. Amanda had been on the job little more than a week before August 5.

On that day, Amanda offloaded the van and signed off that all the children were out of the vehicle and in the school. Petra Rodriguez signed off, confirming that all the children were accounted for. Neither Petra nor Amanda followed procedure. Neither of them checked to be certain that all the children were accounted for. To me, this is unforgivable. They didn't check the van or the classroom for the physical presence of each and every child. I find it especially unconscionable considering that Petra was running the two-year-old room where Haile should've been. She signed off that all the children were present without calling the roll or doing a head count. What's worse, she later admitted to the police that in the past, she'd *never* physically checked to see that each child who was supposed to be present was in fact where he or she was supposed to be. Petra will have to deal with her own demons the rest of her life for doing things her way and not the correct way. She skipped important and necessary steps of procedure that were designed and proven to be effective to assure the safety of little ones in pre-school. Her neglect of the rules led to the death of Haile Brockington. She also ruined my life and damaged many others. I hope I can forgive her. Haile's death in the van would not have occurred had Michelle, the regular teacher, or Patricia, her assistant, been watching over the two-year-olds that day. They would have noticed that Haile was missing and paid attention when Haile's older sister and some staff inquired as to her whereabouts that morning. The answer Petra gave the staff was that Haile must be sick and at home. My director was specifically asked about Haile and she did not check; she didn't follow up. The morning of August 5, the Department of Children and Families showed up around ten o'clock to follow up on a report from a parent about a one-year-old with scratches. Scratches sometimes happen in pre-schools. They are a fairly common occurrence when babies are together. They tend to grasp at things, and if their nails aren't trimmed, it's possible for one baby to scratch another. There is no malice, it's just reaching out. The DCF finished quickly, saying there was no fault on the part of the school, and left. How I wish that someone had glanced into the van when passing through the parking lot. Haile might have been OK at that point, and if she was, there'd have been a chance an adult might have found her before it was too late.

What confuses me more than anything about the accounts told about that day is that Amanda Inman apparently took that van, with Haile on board, to drive a staff member home and then went on her lunch break. How did they not see that little girl in the back?

It was a busy day at New Delray. The state Department of Health showed up a little after noon for an inspection, and all attention then focused on the inspectors. Petra left the supervision of the two-year-olds to other staff and deserted the room. The inspection would have covered all of the common areas of the school. They would check for safety violations with chemicals, anything construed to be a danger, cleanliness, scheduled timeframes, and the like. They'd check the temperature of the food being served, food storage, functionality in the bathrooms, just about everything. In a school the size of New Delray, it could take two investigators a couple of hours, and the director had to be present. The amazing thing is that the transport vehicles are included in this type of inspection. I will never know how they inspected that van with Haile in it without seeing her. The inspectors signed off on the vehicles, along with everything else concerned, rating us with compliance. I'm not sure how a baby left in a van is within compliance, but they gave it to us. Let's recap. Neither Petra nor Amanda checked the rosters or did a head count to be sure all the children entrusted to Katie's Kids who had come on the school van were accounted for: they did no count in or by the van, and no count in the classroom.

Petra is asked about Haile's whereabouts by staff, who had been asked by Haile's older sister about where her sister was. Petra says Haile must be sick at home and didn't come to school.

The Department of Children and Families pays a visit around ten o'clock, passing by the van when they go into and out of the school, and nothing is noticed. They weren't checking out vans, though; they'd come on other business.

At noontime, the Department of Health carries out a two-hour inspection that is supposed to include all transport vehicles. When those investigators were at the school, Haile might still have been alive!

Everything about that fateful day was a cluster-fuck of epic proportions from the word "go."

South Florida in August can be like a furnace. Poor Haile was strapped to a booster seat in that roasting van where the temperature could only go up as the day progressed. We'll never know if she fell asleep or sweated it out, waiting for someone to come and get her. Did she know she was in mortal peril? Was she crying for help? Did she struggle to get free? I can guarantee you, I have had living nightmares about those questions ever since. I cannot remove the image of that child slowly dying. There's not a day that goes by without her coming to mind, and sometimes, in weaker moments, I openly lament and castigate myself for failing to protect her at the moment when she most needed it.

There is no way I can forgive myself for what happened. Despite working with people in intensive counseling and others, there's been only one person since the tragedy who just held me and let me cry my heart out. She didn't tell me to suck it up and move on or to get over it. She knew deep in her soul that I felt I'd left myself in that van to die. This person empathized with my reactions. She knows who she is, and knows I love her for it.

Haile Brockington was a beautiful, two-year-old little girl with a decidedly passive personality. In a school full of hyper personalities, she blended into the background. The only time she was upset was when she was first separated from her older sister. Separation anxiety at that age is understandable. She never got into trouble, and since she was so quiet, she tended to go unnoticed. I'm sure you've heard the old adage of the squeaky wheel getting the grease; well, Haile never needed grease. A friendly smile was more than enough for her. Her pretty brown eyes would sparkle every time you smiled at her, and she'd give you her cute-little-girl gap-toothed grin.

Haile and her siblings spent the majority of their lives removed from their mother's care. The Department of Children and Families had them placed with their grandma most of the time. Whenever they were returned to their mother, we had a nightmare on our hands figuring out where to go to pick them up. Often they'd be at a cheap motel, as their mother didn't have a permanent address. I'm sure Mom was trying her best, but I felt sorry for those kids.

Patricia felt very close to Haile, since she had a personality much like N'gozi's. They played well together and loved to learn whatever was offered, which is typical of inquisitive and bright children. They'd play quietly at recess and not bother a soul. They had excellent manners. Haile would eat the meals provided her like any truly hungry child. She didn't care what it was, as long as it filled her up. She was easy. She was sweet. She was loved by all. She is missed terribly.

Haile's body was not discovered until that afternoon, when the children were boarding the van to go home. Another child saw her first. She screamed to the adults that there was a baby in the van and it didn't look right. Lord, have mercy! What a sight for that poor girl to see. She began screaming, "She's dead, she's dead," and then ran out of the van in tears. Petra Rodriguez was at the front of the van loading an infant when the girl who found Haile banged by her.

Patricia and Vicky, another of our teacher's aides, were standing together outside the van door in confusion when Petra started screaming for someone to call 911. Vicky ran into the building for the phone and called. Patricia got into the van to see who'd hurt themselves, because she had CPR first-aid training. Petra jumped out of the van and took the phone. She was panic-stricken and screaming, but Patricia still didn't know what the problem was.

Amanda Inman was also in the van, and she got to the slumped-over Haile first. She unbuckled the harness and picked her up. Patricia thought someone had passed out until Amanda handed the little girl to her. She stood there holding that poor little body in her arms, recognizing Haile at the same instant that she realized that she was dead. Even so, she laid her gently down and checked for a pulse. There was none. In agony, Patricia scooped her back up and held Haile to her heart. Someone handed Patricia the phone. The 911 operator was telling her to perform CPR, but Patricia, fighting her emotions, explained that the little girl was dead and that rigor mortis had begun to set in. There was nothing she could do. Haile was already in the hands of God.

Petra came back out of the school and told Amanda to move the van off to the side of the building. Everyone was crying uncontrollably. Patricia pulled the doors shut on the van and held Haile as Amanda moved the van as Petra had asked. Patricia continued to hold that poor baby, whom she'd adored, and wept for her. She refused to let anyone take her until the paramedics arrived. She wanted her body to be handled with the utmost dignity.

Patricia was hesitant to hand Haile over, even to the paramedics. She felt so guilty that she'd let this beautiful little girl down. She knew she should have known something was wrong. She should have pushed harder to be with the two-year-olds that day. If she had been adamant, Haile might still be alive. She was devastated by self-imposed culpability. She hugged Haile tight as her soul mourned until the body was forcibly taken from her arms.

Patricia sat down on the ground by Haile's body, refusing to leave her side even when told that she must. She wanted to watch over what was left of Haile until the parents arrived. After twenty minutes sitting by that tiny, shrouded frame, the police finally made her leave what was now a crime scene. Patricia was crushed by guilt. For the rest of her life, she'd feel somehow responsible, just like me.

She went back into the school to help the police locate Haile's records so they could contact the parents, but the phone numbers for them weren't working. The shock was wearing off and anger was setting in. Why had Haile been left? What in the hell was that little girl doing all the way in the back row? She should have been near the front because of her age and size. The driver should have known that. Even if Haile had fallen asleep, if she had been in the proper row, Amanda would have seen her. Why the hell had Petra refused to let Patricia train Amanda? She would have understood protocol better. Why were some people so damn petty when it came to hierarchy? If Patricia had been able to show Amanda the ropes, Haile might be alive today. Amanda obviously hadn't been taught properly. And she knew nobody had done their jobs. Everybody had dropped the ball. Only this ball was not a plaything; it was a beautiful little girl. It was Petra's responsibility to physically check that van before she signed off, and she hadn't bothered to. Patricia was furious, and for the first time in her life, she was experiencing true hate!

She was determined that the police should know the truth. She wasn't going to hide or prevaricate. She loved working for Katie's Kids, and it was being torn asunder. She'd stand up and relay the truth, regardless of repercussions from her supervisor, Petra, New Delray's director.

Shanelle Harp had been a driver for Katie' Kids for two years. She had earned her CDL at my insistence. I paid for her training. She showed up at New Delray that day following her Wexford runs, just to see if they needed any help with their new driver. She arrived to a scene of bedlam. She drove through the throng around the parking lot, confused. Shanelle is a mother of eight children herself, and the sight of that tiny form being worked on by paramedics tore at her heart and terrified her. She knew something horrible had happened. She was a parent, too. She had kids enrolled at New Delray. She was frantic until she knew her children were safe. It could've been her own child lying there.

She, like Patricia, had children in class with Haile; her daughter Alexis and adopted son Xzavion. Unbelievably, she learned the identity of the dead child from her two-year-old daughter. She had charged into the school to check on Alexis and Xzavion, oblivious of the heated crowd threatening with rocks. She'd bulled her way into the room and swept Alexis up into her arms and held her tight. Alexis was crying and saying that Haile was dead. "She's gone, she's just gone." Shanelle was shocked and asked how she knew it was Haile. Her daughter hiccoughed and snuffled into her shoulder that the big man in the suit had told her.

Thank God the big man in the suit wasn't in the classroom, because Shanelle would've ripped his head off if he had been. Nobody should be telling two-year-olds anything so serious without their parents or a guardian being present. It is ridiculous to think otherwise. Children are very sensitive, and the detective should've known better. In the rush to help the other children and staff, though, he was soon forgotten.

Most of the parents had retrieved their children. The children of parents without transportation were to be shuttled to a nearby church, where they'd wait for a ride home. The crowd went ballistic when the staff began to appear outside. Rocks and bricks were hurled at them, regardless of the children who accompanied them. Shanelle can be ferocious, and she dared the crowd to stone her. They backed off when they saw she was like a lioness defending her cubs. The message was clear: *Nobody's going to throw anything at my babies!* She could work off some fear and aggression at the same time, though, if they had. She had seen tiny Haile, her skin darkened — by the heat, most likely — and it shook her to the core. She was traumatized by her daughter's despair and was willing to take on any comers. The crowd prudently let her be.

Shanelle has always been one of my biggest supporters and knew this was going to destroy me psychologically and financially. She always said she was impressed by my ability to fight the odds in life and was worried that this would kill me. I would've thought she was right.

Upon landing from New York at West Palm Beach International, I called the staff to have a compulsory meeting. I wanted to know exactly what had happened and how everyone was coping. The majority were a mess, as you'd imagine. We met at the Boynton School. We all talked. They cried. We shook our heads in disbelief. Everyone kept talking about the two-hour meeting we had held just before I left. Everyone just kept crying—that is, everyone but me. They kept saying that I had told them before I left to make sure they swept the vans to confirm that all the children had gotten off.

I sat in that meeting devastated, weakened, in shock, and hoping I'd wake up from the nightmare my professional life had become. I wasn't mad yet. Assuredly, I was terribly hurt and confused. With all of the safeguards implemented by the state and that I had preached upon, I could not fathom how this could have happened. There are so many checks and balances mandated under state law to which we had to conform. It should have been impossible for this to occur. The problem, as it turned out, was complete and utter disregard for the rules. "Human error" is a term I never want to hear again. Laziness is more like it.

I asked everyone to write down their recollections from the day before. That's how I learned that some staff had asked Petra about Haile early in the day and that she hadn't bothered to check. I was told she rode around on her high horse ignoring them, and as far as I'm concerned, she didn't get knocked off that damn horse nearly hard enough. She should have gone to jail instead of just getting probation. She flagrantly abused her position as a pre-school director entrusted with the care of children, and because of it, a child died. I fired her that same day. Her firing will never be enough for me.

Amanda Inman, the new driver, didn't come to the meeting. She was probably hiding underneath whatever rock she'd climbed out from under to ruin Katie's Kids and my life. To this day I have never met Amanda Inman in person, ever! I did learn more about her aside from the recommendations that brought her to us while I was on vacation. I learned that she had a criminal record and that she should never have been recommended, let alone hired. What a discovery that was. And it was something that Petra Rodriguez should have been aware of. This was compounded when it turned out that Petra Rodriguez herself should never have been approved for her own job! I was getting mad, but this emotion could not supplant my devastation. I had promised to protect children, and Haile had died at my school. I will never get over it.

The tortured staff concluded that meeting wondering what their futures would hold. Katie's Kids was in serious trouble, and it was not going to get better anytime soon; they felt sure of that. I knew I was at risk of losing everything. I had financed everywhere I could for New Delray and mortgaged everything else. I was terrified.

When we emerged from the meeting, the newspaper reporters swarmed over us like particularly nasty bees. They were vicious. The television reporters were waving their cameras like halberds and microphones like spears. I was sweating and shaking in the August heat, because the media wanted my head. Shanelle and the others tried to shelter me as best they could, but my demise at the hands of the press was inevitable. I was the owner of Katie's Kids, and everyone wanted my blood.

It was time to get legal help. I realized that as I drove away. I didn't have a clue about what to do, and I needed to call a lawyer. Betty Resch was a friend, and she was the only lawyer knew. I wasn't sure of how receptive she would be, since her specialty is family law and I saw myself as the guilty party. I had let a family down. Would Betty take my call?

She told me to come straight to her office. I drove there directly. She held me for a minute, and I cringed. She knew how serious I was about caring for children and understood my devastation. She asked me if I had Haile's parents' phone number. I told her my staff didn't have a working number for the family, because they were staying in a hotel. I phoned some of the staff and soon had the right number. This was a call I didn't want to make. What was I supposed to say? Nothing I could say or do would make things right. I couldn't bring their daughter back, but I felt an apology was needed. This to me wasn't good enough, but it's all I had to give them. I would rather have been on that van than Haile. I wished that God could have taken me instead of her. Trembling inside and out as my attorney held my hand, I made the phone call.

I needed to speak with both parents and express my regrets. The first person I spoke with was Haile's mother. I told her how sorry I was for her loss. I asked what I could do for her. She said, "Nothing right now." She didn't yell or scream or curse at me. I wanted her to. I wanted her to at least tear me up, just as I was tearing myself up. She was calm and collected. Then, as an aside, she asked me if I had a picture of Haile for the newspapers, since she didn't. I said I could probably find one. She then accepted my apology and handed the phone to Haile's father. I told him I was sorry for his loss and asked if there was anything I could do to help. He accepted the apology without comment and then said good-bye. I gave them my cell phone number and said they could call me anytime, twenty-four hours a day, seven days a week, and I'd answer.

That was the most surreal conversation I had ever had in my life. It seemed that I was trapped in the Twilight Zone, and I felt like my stepfather when he apologized for raping me as if it was nothing. *Sorry your baby died, talk to you later.* It was totally devoid of emotion on their part. When I got off the phone, I lost it. I wasn't sure who I was or what was going on. Betty assured me I had done the right thing and held me again through this emotional storm.

When I calmed down, I was onto Haile's parents' request for a photograph before I left the lawyer's office. Here was something I could immediately accomplish. A week before, a photographer had come to the pre-school and taken pictures of all the New Delray children. I called the company asking them to please expedite our order. The pictures arrived the next day, including copies for Haile's family free of charge. That is the picture that everyone relates to when they think of little Haile; with her blue shirt and Mona Lisa smile, she stole the hearts of millions.

How ironic it was to learn much later from the head director that Amanda Inman had brushed Haile's hair for that picture.

At the schools, we tried to get back to normal as best we could, but it wasn't easy with the swarming press and determined inspectors surrounding us. They seemed set on flaying Katie's Kids to the bone, beginning with me. Everyone was convinced I was a bad guy. My lawyer had recommended I lie low from the press until all the legal battle lines were drawn. My insurance was in for a huge hit, and so was the company.

Every agency that had in the past consistently touted my excellence and that of my schools began to find fault. I lost one accreditation, and others seemed to be in jeopardy. Everyone was on a witch hunt. I held on for the kids.

The Early Learning Coalition was at the front of the pack. They had a meeting scheduled for mid-August and decided to put me on the agenda. They were primed for a lynching, and Katie's Kids and I were to be hung out to dry. I had forty-eight hours' notice that I was expected to be at the ELC session. The coalition didn't even observe common decency by notifying me that they wanted me to appear; the only reason I learned about it, even at the last moment, was thanks to a heads-up from a reporter. It seemed like I was spending a lot of time being surprised by news crews.

One of the newscasters asked me what I thought of being reviewed by the ELC at a meeting coming up in two days. I gave her a blank stare while thinking, *Just what are you talking about?* I was already quite uncomfortable with her, because she never really asked to put her hands down my shirt to hook up her microphone. I was so protective of my personal space. When you've been sexually abused, you have very strict physical boundaries when dealing with anyone, especially strangers. With all the reporters shoving microphones into my clothing lately, I'd become a basket case. I was already upset about the newscaster's hands, and now I realized that she was the bearer of some pretty bad news.

Before she could go any further, I took off, tearing away the microphone and throwing it to the ground. I headed into the parking lot to call my attorney from the security of my car. I asked

Betty about the meeting, when it was, and what the coalition was deciding about Katie's Kids. She said she didn't know anything about it but that she'd get to work finding the answers and call me back as soon as she had them. I sat there ensconced in my car, waiting for a death knell. This could not be good.

My attorney was wonderful. She had taken me on out of the kindness of her heart and didn't ask for a retainer. I felt bad for her, because she had so much to do. Between talking back and forth with the detectives, health department officials, and insurance adjusters, she also had to handle all the news media. She used a huge binder to keep track of all the news-people she and her staff had to deal with every day.

When it came down to the nitty-gritty, Betty told me it would be a very good thing to pay for Haile's funeral. She knew I was stressed and stretched to the limit and that I couldn't afford to pay her *and* for the funeral, so she suggested that I concentrate on just the funeral. I am thankful for such loving advice and direction.

Betty found out the ELC meeting was to be on August 19. On that day, I was so scared that I became physically ill. I had lost about fifteen pounds in less than two weeks, and I was skinny to start with. Now I looked anorexic. Betty accompanied me, and I remember her handing me a Slim-Fast to drink when we arrived. I told her I didn't want it, that I wanted to feel the pain of not eating. I didn't feel I had a right to eat. I wanted to die inside, and I needed to feel physical pain to remind me that I was alive and that this was all very real.

Several of my students' parents spoke emotionally on my behalf. They described the wonderful learning environment at my schools. They said they would keep their children with me, because I ran great schools and they were not afraid of me. I spoke on behalf of myself and all the children I wanted to continue to help. I begged for the life of my school. None of what we said was good enough. The coalition wanted my blood. This was a high-profile case and they, like every other agency, wanted the nightmare to go away. I was expendable. The Department of Health and the Department of Children and Families hadn't completed their investigations, let alone issued reports, and yet coalition officials at the meeting said that my pre-school wasn't safe. They cancelled all funding for New Delray, a quarter-million dollars that were needed for the underprivileged kids enrolled at my school.

The coalition isn't the agency that determines whether or not a school is safe. That's the job of the Department of Health. The coalition took away my funding anyway. About two weeks later, the state's Department of Health declared me to be a safe pre-school operator, stating that the two employees deemed responsible for the Haile Brockington death had not followed protocol. The clean bill of health from the state came too late.

When the Early Learning Coalition pulled my funding, I knew New Delray was finished. I closed it a little more than a month later, on September 30. With that completed, I knew I now faced a battle to keep the three remaining pre-schools alive. The Coalition was making an example of me, and there was little or nothing that I could do to change its determination.

The state, in its report, made it clear that I did not run unsafe pre-schools! Unfortunately, my schools and I were the victims of two employees who didn't fulfill the obligations of their jobs. Both Petra Rodriguez and Amanda Inman were fired. I desired that both should be prosecuted for their dereliction of duty.

After New Delray closed, I warned Barbara about my fears that our own bankruptcy would be inevitable. All our finances were tied up with Katie's Kids, so we would have to file personally along with filing for the business. This would be hard on both of us. We had always paid all our bills punctually. We were both upstanding individuals, and we were being dragged through the mud. Barbara was not happy, and neither was I.

We had to make recompense and would lose everything, all because of "human error" — a term I've come to hate. Barbara knew of an attorney who had helped a school district colleague through bankruptcy and we decided we'd better call. We owed more than three million dollars. Barbara's salary as a teacher wasn't going to go far when faced with an amount like that, and it looked like I was going to go broke. There was no way to avoid filing.

We went to meet with the bankruptcy attorney. He knew exactly who we were, since my name had been headlined in so many news reports and in the newspapers. The attorney said that filing for bankruptcy wouldn't be a problem. At first, we were going to file Chapter 11 for the business, because I wanted to keep the schools open. Chapter 11 bankruptcy would have allowed Katie's Schools to continue creating income to pay off a portion of the debt we owed to our creditors.

But in tears, Barbara asked me to shut the schools down, pleading with me to leave with her so we could start our lives over in a new place. I told her I wouldn't do that and that we needed to think of the children, that I was going to fight to keep Katie's Kids alive. I thought I understood where she was coming from, but I had to do what I believed was right. I continued my efforts to keep the pre-schools running. By then, Barbara wouldn't allow me to even speak of the business. She couldn't bear the stress of it any more. Our relationship of so many years was headed for the rocks.

For me, the stress was worse at home than at work. Between the two, I never got a break. Whenever I was on the phone with staff, Barbara felt the need to get out of the room. We were both frazzled to the bone, but I was determined to keep the schools alive. I had put all my heart and soul into the pre-schools and shutting them down felt akin to killing myself.

It became clear that we would lose our home. We had taken a loan against the house in Lake Worth to raise funds for buying the Boynton and Margate schools. The loss of our home was devastating. We'd had it since 2001, and it held so many memories for us. My father and I had spent six months renovating the place after Barbara and I bought it. I'd cared for my first pre-schoolers there. With Barbara I lived there happily, no longer stumbling over the memories of my childhood horrors. But our lives as happy homeowners were over.

Due to the trauma of Haile's death, the business collapsing, and the emotional toll of it all, Barbara decided that after the bankruptcy, she would leave Florida and take a teaching position overseas. She found one in Ulan Bator, the capital of Mongolia. That sounded about as far away from Florida as the moon.

Barbara and I had been together since I was eighteen. We had always been close, even in these tough days and through all the stress surrounding Haile's death, the news frenzy, the struggle to save the schools, the bankruptcy, and the likely loss of our home. Barbara had given me a life when she whisked me out of Boston. Now it seemed she needed to escape from me and our troubles.

I was losing my best friend and the only person on whom I could truly rely. Barbara had given me so much love, emotional support, and advice all these years. She had put up with me for so long. She was leaving, and I would be alone again. I felt abandoned. I feel responsible for this, because she is a truly wonderful person, and she shouldn't have had to go through everything that happened to us and to Katie's Kids. We had been through a lot together. I had spent my whole adult life with her, and I'd miss her.

Katie' Kids struggled through the rest of the school year. I knew we were headed for bankruptcy soon because of New Delray closing down. Finances were further compromised by parents who continued to send their kids to us but who couldn't afford the fees. They had never paid. I had gotten them special funding so their children could go at all. And no new children came. The other schools were flooded with inspectors of various levels trying to catch me doing something wrong, but they were never able to come up with anything. At this point, they were just trying to create problems where there were none. We finished the year bruised and battered and, to my relief, intact.

One day, during summer school in June 2011, the director of Boynton told me that a white couple wanted to enroll their two-year-old daughter at the facility for summer camp and that if everything through the summer worked out, she would continue with us in the upcoming school year. I told her to do the interview. I didn't think the parents would follow up anyway when they learned about the racial demographics for the school. It was everything but white.

The mother was adamant that she wanted to talk with me and asked for me by name. Speaking with the school director, I said that something wasn't quite making sense, because no one had referred this couple and that was generally how we got new children: parents talking to parents. Why did she want to speak specifically to me?

When we met the parents, some of their questions were unlike any I'd experienced in such an interview. It seemed a bit weird! I answered everything they asked as I normally did, but I couldn't help but think it was a bit odd that they wanted to know about our hiring policies. My gut was telling me there was something seriously wrong. They asked if it would be OK to introduce me to the girl's grandparents. This was not unheard of, but it was just not the way things usually unfolded. I told them that it wouldn't be a problem at all and I'd be happy to. This was in keeping with our open-door policy with family.

I walked them out, and it was like, oh, surprise, surprise, here are the grandparents! What did these people think, that I was Booboo the Fool? Chris Hansen was standing there, beautifully coiffed and suited. Was I not supposed to recognize him because I'm black, or was I just supposed to be stupid? I'd always loved Chris Hansen's undercover reports for *Dateline NBC*. It was immediately apparent to me that the parents had been filming me through the whole interview and that the stage was set for act two.

One of the staff freaked out when she realized I'd been on camera through the entire interview and was still being taped. Once the remaining staff outside caught on, they shoved me back into the building. The camera was hanging from the father's neck. I didn't know what to do. I am not a criminal. I had no reason to hide anything, so I refused to hide. So what did I do? I walked back outside and approached a woman who looked she was the person in charge. Robbie Gordon is a producer for *Dateline*. I told her I had no qualms about talking to them, but this wasn't the time or the place, because I had children to take care of. She handed me her card and prepared to leave, assuming she was getting the brush-off.

They left, but I couldn't stop thinking about Robbie Gordon. In the few moments that we'd had together, basically just exchanging calling cards, I had felt an instantaneous connection to her. Everyone warned me to not speak with these news-people from New York City, because they could turn the story into whatever they pleased. Yes, that was true, but I wanted our story to be out there. I wanted to bring awareness to the circumstances of Haile's death, because I never wanted to hear that it had happened again.

I decided I would call Robbie Gordon. Before I made that call, a quote from childhood came to mind. It's rather simple, but it says so much: "If you don't stand for something, you will fall for anything." I needed to act on my intuition to help. I waited about twenty minutes before dialing the number for Robbie's cell phone. When she answered, I told her I didn't want to talk to her over the phone and that we should meet in person. Robbie said she was so glad that I had called, because they were prepared to run a story without me. I told her I wanted to tell her the whole truth. She told me she was almost back at the Fort Lauderdale International Airport, but she had a plan. She'd send the undercover crew to the next location and catch a cab back to Palm Beach County to talk to me in person. And she did.

Her taxi pulled up to the school about an hour later. I couldn't help but wonder how much that taxi must've cost. It is weird how your brain works. Who cares how much it cost? An interview with her might have cost me everything!

When she got out of the cab, I was scared. I didn't know if I was doing the right thing. Admitting my disgust over the careless state inspection could be devastating to me and my floundering schools. The state of Florida might not take it kindly if I ratted on their inspectors. I shook Robbie's hand and told her I had a story for her, and that after I told it, I would be finished with the pre-school business. I don't think she really listened right then. She was probably busy thinking about what to ask me, although she had probably worked out her line of questioning in the cab.

I took her to the VPK classroom. I sat there looking around at this room that my dad and I had so lovingly refurbished, knowing that if I did this interview it wouldn't be long before it was gone. I could smell the familiar odors of new books, little kids, Elmer's glue, and old coffee, and realized there was a new aroma: that of my own fear. Parents were picking up their kids from the class and they hugged me or made a point to smile at me to show their unconditional support. They knew I wasn't a monster. Robbie was beginning to catch on.

I told her everything that had happened. It took considerable time, and she was very patient with me. The one piece of information she was really interested in was that the Department of Health had been there that day and had signed off that they had checked the van. Robbie asked me to send her the report, which I later did. She told me how glad she was that I had called; otherwise, *Dateline* would've portrayed me much differently. Robbie and I spoke in calls back and forth for a couple of weeks. The waiting game began.

In the meantime, the local NBC *Channel 5 News* did an interview with me about finding insurance coverage. That was when I first met Katie LaGrone for real. She's an investigative reporter at the station. She used to tease me that I was more famous than she was. I told her I was not famous! I was infamous!

My insurance carrier had settled with Haile's parents for two million dollars. Katie covered the story. My liability policy was for twenty times the hundred-thousand-dollar norm. I had a lot of insurance. If my schools ever messed up, I wanted the beneficiaries to be happy. Well, we had screwed up royally, but I don't know if it made the parents happy. Two million dollars would not have made me happy had I lost a child. My liability coverage was then cancelled. Katie's Kids was no longer insurable.

The news reporters reappeared on the scene and would follow the vans full of kids. For me this was too much. It was dangerous for all those babies. The van drivers could become defensive, and that might cause a greater tragedy than the one we had on our hands already.

The Department of Health kept harassing us, because they knew they had screwed up. With the pressure from reporters and officialdom, I decided I had no choice but to close down the schools. That was June 30, 2011: the last day of my life as I knew it. I was going to have to start over again. But where?

I called Robbie Gordon at *Dateline*. She had told me to keep in touch if anything big happened. This seemed pretty damned big to me. I told her I had shut down everything, including me.

There was a shocked pause on the phone before Robbie spoke. *Dateline* had been working for a very long time on a story about criminal pre-school owners, and I was an important part of it—a good part. I was to be the gem in a pile of rocks. She told me she had just recently spoken by phone with the Department of Children and Families, telling them how wonderful I was and that I had the best pre-schools they'd seen in their cross-country travels. This was such a compliment for me to hear, but it had come too late. It was far, far too late. It didn't matter now.

I had become the whipping boy, and no one wanted to see the whipping end. Somebody had to pay for what had happened, and nobody was particular about the facts or who took the blame. I was the owner, and therefore I was guilty. It became about me and not the director who hadn't bothered checking the bus or thinking to check later on when asked if she knew where Haile was. Neither was it about the driver who, despite a criminal record, had that very day been approved by the state. That pair didn't have to take the heat.

I closed the facilities on June 30, 2011. I went in and swept floors and cleaned toilets. I restacked books and straightened the supply shelves. I toiled over those schools to leave them presentable, and I died inside. I was preparing my babies for burial.

8. Emotional Plummet

I hit rock bottom and landed hard. Battered and bruised, I buried my children and was confounded. Night sweats and night terrors of the sort a three-year-old has prevented me from getting sleep, and for the first time in many years, I thought I'd be better off dead. I was back at the foot of the mountain and staring into a deep pit.

Barbara and I were lost to each other. I had dragged us down into the depths, drowning our long-term relationship, and there were no life preservers to buoy us up. The losses of our home, business, and dignity, coupled with so much pressure from reporters and my relapse into depression, became far too much for Barbara to endure. Who could blame her? I couldn't deal with it either. I ran away and left her. I was at the edge of the pit.

I began hanging out with someone new and her crowd. They were a horrible influence, just what I needed. Alcohol came into my life. For the first time, I had a drink, then a second, and then several more. I don't remember how many. I got drunk, and for quite a long time I drank almost every night. Alcohol blotted everything out. I didn't have to think, feel, or react to any emotions when I drank. I could just float in a distilled-liquid haze and just be.

I started smoking cigarettes too. The ceremony of the lighter attracted me. I'd cough and sputter, and my addictive personality drew me right in. There is a very ritualistic quality to smoking that distracted me from dwelling on the misery I felt. Anyone who smokes knows exactly what I mean. Anyone who hasn't thinks I'm nuttier than they did before. That's fine. It truly is a process: holding the pack with its crinkling cellophane wrap just so, tapping out the cigarette, placing it precisely between your lips, grasping the lighter at the proper angle while cupping the flame to protect it from rogue breezes, then the roll of the metal against flint sparking the flame, the crackle of tobacco as it ignites, and at last, that first deep inhale. Ah, success! The smoke calms my nerves and drives a nail into my coffin! I knew I shouldn't do it, but I didn't care. It made me feel better, even if only for just a few moments. Anything destructive was right up my alley during those eight months.

There was one really good thing that came out of the new relationship and all my self-flagellation. We were on the beach down in Key West watching the sunrise when I was presented with that recognizable picture of Haile and told to show what I was feeling. My system finally hit the critical point and I boiled over. The tears started dripping and then gushing from my eyes. They had been dry such a long time—most of my life, really. I distinctly remember the salty, hot, sticky trails down my cheeks from the roiling tears. They were a nasty combination of lost innocence, guilt, and grief.

It was a Sunday morning. I decided to call Robbie Gordon in New York. It wasn't even eight o'clock, but I called anyway and left a message. I was ready for the next step. Robbie called me right back to set up the interview with Chris Hansen at *Dateline*. We scheduled it for that week.

Gordon, Hansen, and the camera crew flew to Florida and met me at the shell of what had been the Wexford School. I couldn't believe how depressing that empty building was. There was no laughter, no children, no tears, nothing.

By now I'd had plenty of experience with film crews. They seemed so unfeeling and invaded my personal space, the fingers of strangers slipping under my shirt to hide microphones. Robbie listened to me explain how uncomfortable I could be with men because of the sexual abuse. I warned her that if Chris came down hard on me, I would psychologically disappear. She stopped everyone in their tracks and took Chris aside.

From that point on, I felt like a treasured china vase from the Ming Dynasty. Everyone handled me with great care and consideration. My tensions subsided and I began to feel more comfortable. They let me settle the microphone myself. They slowed down and asked my permission at every step. It was amazing. I was so appreciative.

Chris Hansen came over to me and took my hand like a good father would and drew me aside. He looked at me with those piercing, inquisitive eyes he's famous for and spoke in that uncompromisingly smooth voice of his, and he made me feel safe. For a split second, I was transported back in time to the courtroom in Massachusetts, staring into the eyes of the kindly judge who'd granted me freedom from my stepfather. Then I blinked, the comforting vision cleared away, and I was back in the center of my current nightmare.

Chris promised not to scare me. He swore he'd be kind and unthreatening. He kept those promises. We talked for a long while about my life and all of my turmoil. He promised that during the interview, I could stop at any point if I started to feel uncomfortable. He was the first male stranger I had been around in years, and yet I was relaxed with him.

The interview began. He asked about my past and the toil it had taken to get where I was. We talked about everything at length. It took more than an hour. We discussed my schools, the state regulations, and how bad I felt. It tore me wide open.

That was the day I found out about Amanda Inman's criminal history. *Dateline* had done a background check on her as the state of Florida should have. I was so shocked that I became tongue-tied. Chris asked if I would have hired Amanda if I'd known. My response was an emphatic no. That's the first I had learned of the fact that the state had formally approved Amanda on the very day on which Haile died. That is reprehensible to me. I should have been told of her background, and she should not have been approved to drive children.

When Chris told me that Petra Rodriguez also had a record, I was stunned and incensed. I had trusted Petra and given her so much responsibility. I shouldn't have let her guard an old shoe, much less one of my schools. The state had really let me down. I wonder who else they are miserably failing to inform. It's laughable and criminal at the same time. I trusted the government to do its job. Should I have done my own criminal checks? It never would have crossed my mind that I'd need to.

Chris enumerated the list of failures on the state's part that led to the tragic death of Haile Brockington. I am not in the blame game. Despite the state's shortcomings, I take responsibility for my company and always will.

Robbie and I talked for quite a while after the interview. I told her that I wanted to become an advocate for children, but I just wasn't sure of the route I needed to take. She told me that something good was coming out of all of this. Legislators in Tallahassee, led by State Senator Maria Lorts Sachs, were proposing changes to the regulations so that it would now be mandatory in Florida for all pre-school vehicles to have an alarm system that alerts drivers and staff that a child has been left on board. The producer laid a challenge before me. She said I should persuade all fifty states to enact this safety measure in their laws. Robbie asked me to keep in touch.

I sat in that empty school for a long time after all the NBC people left. Wexford was supposed to have been my shining star. It was beautiful. Its classrooms had echoed with joyous laughter and anguished tears. Little minds had been enlightened here and taught how to learn. Social skills were introduced and honed for future friendships. Little bellies were assured two good meals a day, which was so important to so many of the kids whose families were so poor they didn't know where their next meal would come from. The children had laughed and learned and grown. Now there was only silence.

I sat at a little red table on a little red chair, one of many I had chosen so carefully for all the schools. I looked back over the past seven years as I absentmindedly stroked the shiny tabletop. I had made a commitment to myself that I would love, protect, cherish, and teach children. I had done that. I had influenced hundreds of children's lives and futures. I had achieved a meteoric success. I had become a millionaire seemingly overnight. I gently lowered my head to the table and lay there in an ever-expanding pool of sorrow. The tears streamed unchecked. For years after Butch abused me, I had refused to cry. Things for me had changed a lot. Now I couldn't seem to stop crying.

I had achieved everything I ever wanted, but at what price? A beautiful little girl was dead, and I would never get past that fact. I would never be comfortable again with direct responsibility for children. Weeping at that red table, I decided that I would never own, operate, or work for another school. I felt that there would always be a reflection of Haile in tiny, trusting faces.

I wasn't going to be able to handle her picture in my own mind's eye, either. She would always be there, reminding me of lost innocence. My own innocence that was taken at the age of twelve, then again at the age of thirty-one, was gone forever. I would always feel guilty about doing something wrong that resulted in my being abused and causing my stepfather's death. I would always feel guilty about not being there for Haile that day. I would always bear the grief of that innocent little life lost.

I reflected on all the wonderful staff who were now unemployed. I concentrated upon those who I knew felt as badly as I did about Haile. They were numerous, and many would never work in pre-schools again. What a colossal waste. They were innocent of everything regarding Haile's death, but, like me, they continued to feel niggling doubts engendered by what-ifs. Patricia Daniels had quit that day after having held that poor baby's lifeless body until the authorities made her reluctantly give it up. Patricia will never teach again. It's a shame, because she's an amazing teacher. She would remember Haile forever as well—as her son's playmate, as a quiet, loving student, and as the tiny body she had watched over. The good memories were overshadowed by tragedy and guilt.

So much was lost when Haile died. Her poor parents, grand-parents, and siblings would have to move on through life without her. I would carry her memory with regret inside me forever.

I laid my head there for quite a while, just wishing that this nightmare had never happened. I was suffering withdrawals from not seeing my kids. There were no more hugs and kisses from my adoring students, no more green, runny noses and barking coughs that invariably sent me to the doctor, no more praise from parents, no more playing tag on the ice, no more stretching my imagination to curb the high-strung personalities of naughty children, no more of anything that had mattered to me.

The sun had set outside the school, bringing darkness that reflected the blackness in my soul. I stood up, carefully wiped down the table, tucked the chair underneath, and took a last look around. I couldn't think about what would happen next. I didn't really even care if there *was* a next.

My shoes echoed down the deserted hallway as I made my way to the exit. That was the last time I walked the halls of Wexford. As I left, the door to the outside closed with a final bang. I was shut out for good.

I lay in bed that night, restless and anxious because I had been having nightmares about Haile's death for weeks. I couldn't sleep. I didn't want to close my eyes and wonder about her last few hours trapped in the school van. I didn't want to worry anymore about whether she had suffered. I didn't want to see the yellow plastic sheet being raised from her body by the investigators, a scene that was played again and again on the news.

The weeks dragged by, and I still wasn't able to sleep. One night, I'd had enough. I took a handful of pills from my bottle of Xanax and swallowed them. I wasn't really sure if I wanted to die, but I couldn't continue reliving all those horrible thoughts every day, asking the endless what-if questions and enduring so much pain.

The girl I was staying with at the time somehow saw me take the pills. She rushed over to me and tried to make me vomit by shoving her fingers down my throat. I bit her. She kept saying, "Come on, Katie, throw up the pills." She was slapping me and crying, begging me to puke them out. I wouldn't. She dragged me to the car and drove me to Columbia Hospital in West Palm Beach. I was so angry with her. I didn't want to go to an emergency room. I wanted to sleep the night away and possibly end my life. I didn't know for sure, and heading to the hospital, I didn't care. I didn't want to be put away in a lockdown unit for seventy-two hours, something I knew they would do. I had been a professional at this once.

I don't remember being put on a bed in the emergency room. All I recall was being hooked up to heart monitors. Whenever I dozed off, the heart monitor alarm would sound, because my heart rate had slowed below sixty beats a minute. The monitor alarm would startle me awake and I'd jerk upright, which would get my heart rate back up to a safe level. The nurses would rush in to check my vitals, and I would lie back down. I don't remember how many hours this continued. I was a sort of pathetic jack-in-the-box. I also don't remember being taken to the lockdown unit until my vital signs were checked again and I was asked lots of questions that didn't compute very well, considering my drugged mind.

I remember waking up the following day and telling my nurse that this was all a big mistake and that I didn't belong in lockdown. I had only wanted to sleep. I wanted to go home. The nurse explained that she couldn't do anything. I would have to wait until I saw the doctor, who wouldn't be there until much later on. The nurse told me to attend the morning group therapy session. I obliged and went. Some of the patients recognized me. The therapist reminded them that everything in the hospital was confidential. I couldn't even go to a hospital and not be recognized. I was infamous by association, thanks to those two stupid women whose negligent actions had led to Haile's death.

I finally met with a doctor, a woman who wanted answers to plenty of questions. I told her I didn't belong where they'd put me and that I wanted an immediate release. She told me that she wasn't the doctor assigned to me and was merely filling in until the more senior doctor could see me. I got upset. What did it take to see my doctor around here anyway, a suicide attempt? Forgive me; I'd tried that already, hadn't I?

The doctor said I could be discharged in a couple of days if I would sign a seventy-two-hour release. That wasn't good enough for me. I wasn't used to people telling me what to do anymore. I had a fit and told her she had to let me go. The doctor slammed my file shut, said I was out of control and needed to calm down, and that there was no way she would allow me to leave. I ranted at her that she'd be worse if she were in my shoes, shouting that nobody could survive what my life had become.

I wanted to screech like a banshee and throw all the furniture around the room. I wanted to have a temper tantrum like a two-year-old because I couldn't have my way. I wanted to kick and scream and bite and scratch at fate, which had taken away everything I held dear.

Charging for the phone, I yanked the handset from the cradle as nurses descended on me with a hypodermic needle filled with a tranquilizer. I wanted to call for help, but even in my hysteria I realized that there was no one I could call. There was no one for me to rely on. What a horrendous thought. I had no one. The last thing I remember of that episode is being propped up by nurses. When I woke up, I realized that I had been gently restrained to my hospital bed. The remnants of the tranquilizer left me muddled for a while. I knew what kind of room I was in, but I didn't know what year it was.

As a young woman, I'd spent so much time in lockdowns, and that day I seemed to go through a dreamlike regression to those earlier times. I relived stays in other stuffy little rooms where I was forced to reflect on my reactions to traumatic events. As I slipped back into the present, I knew I had to stop doing this and grow up. I had to suck it up and move on. God obviously had other plans for me. I needed to get on with life and quit hiding. I dozed off into a confused dream of yesterdays and todays.

Contrary to what the doctors thought was best for me and some unconscious doubt of my own, I was released from Columbia after the prescribed three-day stay. There was no doubt that I needed help, but I was stubborn and determined to get out and find my way on my own without shrinks.

Here's a definition of insanity I relate to: the repetition of an identical chain of events accompanied by continuous irrational expectation of different outcomes. So yes, I was pretty much insane.

The only thing I had going for me was school. Sometimes people revert to holding onto security blankets. I'd always felt safer at school where Butch couldn't get to me. Now I only had Florida Atlantic University.

One accreditation I'd had for my schools was Quality Counts, awarded by the Early Learning Coalition. They provided teachers in accredited facilities with funding to pay for bachelor's degrees. Ironically, the very organization that had declared New Delray unsafe, pulling the rug out from underneath Katie's Kids and destroying my world, had all along been paying for my university education.

I was enrolled in summer school at FAU but had to withdraw from all my classes. Summer term is short, and I had missed about two weeks. I was failing, because I couldn't catch up on that much missed material. I went to the assistant dean and filed for medical leave. It was granted to me with their sincerest sympathies. I also talked to the assistant dean about what I had to do for fall semester to get back into school. FAU wanted to make sure I was healthy enough to return. They understood the difficulties I'd been through and were willing to help all they could. They gave me a detailed list of requirements for readmission.

If I wasn't in school, what was I going to do? I had to get back into something structured. The only thing to keep me going would be staying busy so I couldn't dwell on the past.

I couldn't be a child advocate until I was vindicated and shown to be someone quite different from who I had been portrayed as in the news media. Nobody was going to want me to help after I'd been depicted as a baby killer. I had to wait until I was proven innocent by *Dateline*. I had to be patient, but I couldn't sit around doing nothing. I was used to working more than ninety hours a week and being around people. I couldn't lounge around with nobody but me for company. What I could do, though, was follow up on the list FAU had given me. I did everything the school requested.

I saw a therapist once a week and was religious about seeing the doctor who became my psychiatrist. I was conscientious about taking my prescribed medications. I asked my therapist to write a letter telling the school I was all right to return in the fall. After receiving it, the assistant dean called me and told me she was going to a meeting where they would decide if I could come back. An hour later, the phone rang again. It was the assistant dean telling me that the committee would welcome me back to the school. I was thrilled. I would also be given access to the disabilities office. This was a wonderful department whose responsibility was to oversee the needs of students with disabilities, helping them to thrive in their university careers. I qualified on many levels, especially with my ADHD and the depression. I was ready to embark on a new challenge—and the sooner, the better.

The beginning of this, my last year at FAU, was dramatic—to say the least. I was an emotional paradox. I wanted so badly to succeed, and yet I couldn't make my broken brain cells work properly. I'm sure my professors thought I was a bit loony. One minute I'd be a pillar of strength, and the next I would practically have a nervous breakdown. Thank the Lord for the disabilities office that arranged for me to take my tests sequestered from other students and distractions. I probably would've flunked out completely if they hadn't done that. The professors, once they learned of my background, really worked with me. They understood when I'd drift off in a funk or was manic about my papers. I'm thankful that I was able to go back. Having a purpose at Florida Atlantic University really saved my life.

During the fall semester, I was in a women's studies class called Women in Business and Power. I was encouraged to go to a conference that was being held on campus. To my surprise, I saw Senator Sachs there. I introduced myself and asked her if she remembered me. She told me no, so I enlightened her, explaining that we had met when she used Katie's Kids for publicity when we installed all of our bus alarms about a year earlier. That was when the senator was proposing the new safety rules requiring alarms, which failed to pass into legislation..

I told her I wanted Haile's Bill to be reintroduced. I had been advocating on the news the need for alarm systems to be required in pre-school transport vehicles on and off for the last year. Lawmakers had failed to pass it by May of 2011. It was important legislation and needed to be passed. I told the senator that I would do anything I could to help her get the legislation through. I gave her my number, and she assured me she would call. She handed me her business card and walked away. I hoped Senator Sachs would keep her promise.

The fall semester seemed to drag by as I struggled with my courses. Some were not very difficult, but others felt close to impossible. I still liked being there, and thank God I did, because the only money I had to my name was from my student loans. I hadn't had a job for over a year, and I was broke. This was a new challenge. I had been a millionaire a little more than a year earlier and could buy what I liked, but now I was counting my change at the school snack bar like any struggling student. Sometimes I'd stand there giggling over the idiocy of it all. Barbara gave me a hand and let me move back in with her (she had not yet left for Ulan Bator). I could not afford housing anywhere else.

It seemed to take forever for *Dateline* to air our interview, and that distracted me from my studies. A public relations firm was helping me with my image; I had contracted them to represent me predicated upon the outcome of the *Dateline* story. I couldn't pursue child advocacy without having my name cleared. Heaven forbid should *Dateline* picture me in a bad light. That would be the final straw, and nobody would be willing to trust me ever again.

Thankfully, before I completely lost my way, I ran into a woman I'd met the previous spring who was also receiving assistance from the disabilities office. We sat and chatted over lunch one day, and she offered to tutor me. She was very bright, and I accepted her offer at once. Lorinda Gonzalez is a pretty little Latina woman with big, brown eyes and long, black hair. She's a great tutor, who owns a company called *Distinctive Writing*.

She worked with me constantly, and she rode around in a motorized wheelchair at full gallop. If you had been there, you would frequently have seen me jogging behind her as she motored her way across the FAU campus. I'd be frustrated and winded all at the same time—frustrated because she brooked no excuses. Terms such as "depressed," "bipolar," or "ADHD" didn't resonate with her. Her disability definitely hadn't affected her brain.

One of the professors I had that fall term was Dr. Kitty Oliver. She taught a women's studies course called Women of Color. She was a fascinating teacher—and she terrified me. She was a small, willowy, black woman with a propensity for hats. They didn't much add to her stature, but they sure gave her panache. She had lively, coffee-colored eyes that could bore right into any and all guilty thoughts of inadequacy. She was a complete stickler about the reports the class wrote, and it was common to see an ocean of red ink covering all the papers she handed back to students. The comments on mine were always a particularly virulent shade of red. It completely flipped me out. I wasn't used to failing. One of my papers took ten revisions! After the ninth try, I was nearly perched in Lorinda's lap as I begged her to help me write it. My writing was just too atrocious to pass muster. She said she'd help.

Lorinda understood my issues but still got a little frustrated with me. If I convince myself that I can't do something, it is rather hard to change my mind. I also can become argumentative. Finally, she told me that there were only two people on campus who really cared about this paper, and one of them was losing interest real fast. It made me stop and think. I had to remember that I wasn't an executive anymore, and I needed help. We eventually got it done.

After my paper was marked and returned to me, the only obvious red on it was the grade. It was an A-minus. I shouted out a big whoop, and the professor jumped as if I'd goosed her. I was so proud of that grade. I had learned perseverance through life experience, and this was proof I could still overcome obstacles.

Barbara and I reestablished our friendship. She was a tremendous help during that last year at FAU. She was always willing to help me with my assignments. Thank goodness she is so smart. There really wasn't a subject she couldn't help me with. I was glad we were talking and hanging out again. She had been by my side for nearly half of my life and will always mean so much. I knew I would miss her badly when she left to teach in Mongolia. To this day, I feel sad about the dismay Barbara and I went through in our relationship. She was my lover, my friend, and the one who will always have a place in my heart. I'm sorry for what happened to us, and I truly hope one day she will be able to forgive me.

When the fall semester ended, I was so relieved to have made it through. How fortunate was I to have a professor like Dr. Oliver, who sticks out in my memory because she was so tough. I learned so much from her, and anytime I write something, I'll always picture her with her hat perched at a rakish angle and leaning over my shoulder.

As the spring semester approached, I began wondering if the Katie's Kids story would ever be aired by *Dateline*. It had been more than seven months since Robbie Gordon, Chris Hansen, and I had met for the interview. Knowing that I needed something to do, Barbara would egg me on to join the school district and teach. I would cringe at the idea because of my promise never to be involved in a school again. I wouldn't be able to do it.

Graduation was now in sight, provided I earned enough credits this final semester to complete my bachelor's degree. It had been fourteen years since I had begun it up in Boston, and here in Florida, it was time to finish strong. I wondered if I would feel more comfortable going north to see my dad's family now that I would be considered educated. Maybe not, though, since I would have to quit smoking first, and drinking would have to be nixed also. The Muhammad clan is very tough. Of course, I didn't count for myself the fact that I had started a multimillion dollar business in my twenties without any help from anyone. Old habits die hard, and a university education was a big habit in my dad's family.

I signed up for the spring semester with a whopping fifteen credits, which meant five classes and five more professorial personalities to decipher. It would be extremely tough. Nevertheless,

I was determined and knew could always get Lorinda to help pick me up when I fell down. Besides, I wasn't doing anything else in the meantime.

I had spoken to an old friend about it. LaTonya—Tonya for short—was going to school as well as holding down a full-time job. Over the past five or so years, we hadn't seen much of each other in person but did manage to keep in touch by phone and on Facebook. Tonya is a very bright lady who missed her calling as a therapist. I have never met anyone who could zero in on a problem I was having the way she could and give me sound advice. I hadn't met anyone else like her, not yet.

She knew how hard I was struggling over the death of Haile and the loss of Katie's Kids. She knew I was lonely because I had never taken time to really invest in friendships. I had always been too busy. Her advice to me was to get out and meet some new people. She badgered me by phone and Facebook to place myself around happy people who did not associate me with their employment or the death of Haile.

So in January of 2012, my resolution to make new friends became a journey into uncharted waters. I had never in my life walked into a public place on my own with the distinct purpose of finding new friends. I am very shy when removed from my own element and comfort zone. Tonya was right in suggesting that I needed to at least try.

I asked around if anyone knew anywhere I might feel comfortable and meet some new people. One place that was recommended turned out to be very close to home, which meant a short escape route if one was needed. I always try to plan ahead, especially since I tend to expect the worst.

I embarked on my first friend-making mission with much trepidation and gritted teeth. I would most likely scare the crap out of anybody who thought to approach me. I probably looked like a snarling tiger when I smiled with my jaws locked shut. Nevertheless, I put myself into the car and drove over.

I was headed to The Bar Lake Worth, in the city of Lake Worth. I had to blink a few times as I came closer to the building, because it was painted an extremely shocking shade of pink. Yes, pink!

The place was packed, and I was really nervous walking through the front door, but I quickly realized that nobody took any notice. There was a floor show in progress, and all attention was turned to the little stage in the middle of the dance floor.

This was perfect. I could drink in the atmosphere and not be too anxious. I bellied up to the bar and when the bartender approached, I asked her for something sweet and strong. She cocked her pretty blonde head to the side, thought for a second, and asked if I liked grapes. I said I did, and she went to mix me a drink.

This was a small, neighborhood bar, full of shadow and surprisingly smoky. This was just what I needed, a place I could practice both of my new vices at once: cigarettes and alcohol. It had one long, L-shaped bar with a couple of dozen bar stools perched along it. There were brick pillars on either side of the dance floor, a pool table shoved up against one wall, and a DJ table shoved up against another. Everyone seemed to be having a great time. There was lots of hooting and hollering because of the show and lots of loud and really bad singing. As each performer finished, there was a big round of applause. It made me smile. Here was a group of people who knew how to have fun. Maybe, just maybe, there was someone here for me to connect with.

Simply being in this place, I began to feel better. I was surrounded by friends-to-be, yet still anonymous. Even though I thought of my past often, my memories would be indistinct and cloudy and sometimes elusive, but of my introduction to The Bar and the times that followed, my memories are clear as a bell.

The bartender came back with my drink; it was a light purple color. She paused in her duties long enough to watch my response to the first sip. Since it was a gasping, sputtering cough, she smiled and waltzed away. Lord, have mercy, it was strong. I had to wipe the spittle from my chin and off the front of my blouse while trying to recover my breath. Thank God, nobody had really noticed. It would have been mortifying. I mopped up the ice cubes that had erupted out of my mouth when I coughed. The bartender sashayed her way back toward me as the mound of napkins I'd stolen out of the holder created a tiny paper mountain. I gave her a wobbly smile, still gasping a bit, and asked what the drink was.

"It's a Grape Nerd," she replied as she removed all the debris in front of me. Maybe it was a typical reaction to her Grape Nerd, because she didn't turn a hair.

"What's your name?" I asked her.

"Missi," she replied with a cheeky grin full of straight, white teeth, much like a particularly generous oyster full of a dozen shiny pearls.

"I'm Kathryn, and that was by far and away the strongest drink I've ever had," I barked at her over the music while still trying to recover my breath.

She gave me that saucy head tilt and said, "I know, it's my specialty! If you want to start a tab, I'll need a credit card." I offered her cash and a brilliant, toothy grin of my own as she sidled away.

I was enjoying the show and the jocularity of the crowd squeezed into the small bar. As I turned away, I caught sight of a smiling image in front of me. The face was beaming, and it took a moment to realize I was looking at my own reflection in the enormous, smoky mirror back of the stocked liquor bottles. My face froze for a moment, and then I smiled even broader. Tonya was right. I had needed to get out.

I peered at myself for a moment. It seemed like forever since I'd seen myself look anything but unhappy. I took in my eyes with their golden irises rimmed by hazel, my broad, inviting smile, the laugh lines bracketing my full, rosy lips, and my wavy black hair severely scraped back into its tiny bun. I don't think I'm bad-looking when I am happy. I needed to work on not appearing to be a sourpuss constantly. More accurately, I needed to work on actually not *being* a sourpuss all the time.

I was distracted by another bartender as she interrupted my view of the mirror. She leaned across the bar and introduced herself. "Hi, I'm Julie, and I don't recall seeing you here before. Is it your first time?"

"Yes," I answered a bit sheepishly, thinking she'd caught me preening in the mirror.

"Well, welcome! What can I get you to refill your glass with?" She gave me a nice, earnest grin and gazed at me from lovely eyes perfectly proportioned in a lovely face. She had light brown hair with natural highlights burnishing brightly under the bar's spotlights. I liked her immediately and hoped we might get a chance to talk a bit.

"I think it's called a Grape Nerd," I replied.

"Coming right up," she said, heading down the bar. She turned back then and warned me, "They can be pretty strong."

I let out a huge crack of laughter and hollered after her, "Yeah, that's the understatement of the century!" I caught my reflection again and felt better than I had in a long time. I felt like I was really welcome here. I turned back to the show.

There were a lot of people packed into tight quarters, like I said, and I was curious about a woman standing sideways to me who seemed to be plopped right in front of all the spectators. She wasn't of an unimposing size. I watched her for a minute before I realized she was shooting video from a tripod and periodically snapping pictures with a rather involved-looking, big black camera with a telephoto lens and a bulky flash on top. She was cheering and applauding as much as the rest, obviously enjoying herself.

I wedged myself behind one of the brick pillars in an effort to dodge any stray photos in my direction. I did not need to get my picture published on the Internet or something, what with a drink in one hand and a cigarette in the other. I don't know who'd take it worse seeing me like that—the public relations people or my dad's family. I didn't know who this woman was working for and didn't want to take any chances.

I'd had enough negative press in the last year and a half to last ten lifetimes. I watched the photographer for a few minutes more after the end of the show. She worked the room like a pro and seemed to know everybody present. Most of them got a hearty hug, a few words, and a bold laugh. She had a nice, open smile and sparkly brown eyes that zeroed in on her subjects. I thought it was funny that she was taking pictures with her eye right up to the back of the camera instead of looking at the LED display. I hadn't seen anybody take pictures that way in a long time, not since I was a little girl, except for the professional newspaper guys with jillions of dollars in equipment who'd hunted me for weeks. I hoped she didn't work for a paper. This woman looked nice, and she seemed comfortable in her own skin. I hoped to meet her, too.

I finished my drink and left a hefty tip for the bartenders. I knew there was no way I could have a third one of those consciousness-killing drinks, or someone would have to call me a cab, pour my drunk ass into it, and hope I could still remember my name, much less my address.

I left The Bar Lake Worth in a better frame of mind than in years. As I drove carefully home, I considered just how long it really had been. I know having Katie's Kids had made me very happy, but personally I couldn't recall seeing myself at any point then and thinking *Wow, I look happy*. Don't get me wrong, I have had plenty of fun and have done some interesting things, but I don't translate that into actually being happy. There have always been too many bad memories overshadowing my emotions to say that. I really needed to lighten up my life somehow. As I fell into bed and lay there muzzily waiting for sleep, I decided I would venture out again soon, just to see what would happen.

The constant wrestling match with the foreclosure lawyers dragged on. My wait for the *Dateline* interview to air was becoming interminable. School was keeping me extremely busy, and I still felt unanchored, like a tiny, wind-tossed boat foundering far offshore in the mighty Atlantic with no land in sight. I couldn't seem to see where I'd been or where I was headed.

As January rolled over into February, I was studying hard and counting the months until I received my degree. Finally, I would feel educated and maybe able to brag to dad's family for once.

On February 18, I decided I would spread my wings again and fly on over to The Bar Lake Worth. I remember the date, because that night changed my life forever. I was just as nervous as the first time. I told myself that at least I might recognize the two friendly bartenders. As I pulled up, the building was just as pink as I remembered, but inside it was not nearly as crowded.

There was a different bartender there than the two I'd met. She'd been there the other time but hadn't served me. I waited for a few minutes as she finished talking to a familiar face at the other end of the bar. It was the woman with the camera. They were laughing and obviously ribbing each other about something. You could tell they were friends and got on well together. The woman had her camera again, and I'd have to make sure she didn't take my picture.

The bartender saw me and acknowledged my presence with a smile in my direction. The other woman didn't look my way. They finished their laugh, and the bartender headed toward me. She crossed her arms, leaned them on the bar, and gave me a pixie smile in a very friendly fashion. She had an extremely short haircut atop a chiseled face leading to a pointed and determined-looking chin. It was a pretty face that openly displayed her warmth, and that chin led me to believe she could be counted on.

"What can I get for you?" she asked.

"A Grape Nerd, please," I replied. She kind of did a double take. I guess it is a sort of signature drink at The Bar.

"Have you been here before?" she asked, a bit confused. I explained about my other visit and she laughed, saying, "It was crazy. I wouldn't have recognized my best friend in here that night." She chuckled as she went down the bar. She must have been very familiar with the customers if she recognized that I was new, but then, the other bartenders had known too. It made me feel good that they paid that much attention to the clientele.

My drink arrived, and this time I cautiously sipped at it. It was strong, but it didn't scorch the lining of my esophagus like the others had. After the bartender asked how I wanted to pay, I asked her name.

"It's Penny. What's yours?" she replied.

"I'm Kathryn." She smiled and hurried off to take care of all the thirsty patrons hanging over the bar rail wanting her attention.

I'd never really done much people watching before. That night I was fascinated by the give and take of various little cliques of people. It was obvious that most of the patrons knew one another. I thought it must be like a small town in there where everybody knew everybody's business. Several people were dancing, and it didn't look like they were all paired up. I was even asked to dance a few times. People grabbed my hands and pulled me onto the dance floor. It wasn't intimidating; if anything, it was a release and fun. It carried me back to when I was little again and my cousins and I were bustin' a move in the living room, showing off our prowess with the latest dances from VH1's music videos. Unfortunately, I don't dance nearly as well as I think I do. My cousins would tear me up. They'd hoot that I couldn't possibly be black, holding their sides as they laughed so hard at my expense. They used to say the only dance I could do was the running man, because I couldn't rock my hips.

I was exhausted, sweaty, and panting when I finally went back for a drink. Lord, I was winded. I discovered I definitely needed to get back to the gym.

Penny hustled up to me and asked if I was ready. I smiled and nodded. Whew, I was tired. That drink went down really quick and satisfyingly. I waved at her and hoisted my glass. She grinned and mouthed to me that it'd be a minute. It was still busy at the bar, but the dense crowd around the floor had begun to disperse.

It was getting late. I was having fun, so I really didn't care. I did keep a roving eye out for the camera lady, just in case. With another drink under my belt, I might just go up and say hi. She had been mingling all evening, taking photos. She really did look nice. She actually looked like she was paying attention to what was conveyed to her. She didn't have the typical social face that reads *I couldn't care less about what you just said.* She'd lean in and listen. It was interesting to watch.

Penny slid the drink across the bar to me and asked, "So, are you having fun yet?"

I laughed now that I could breathe again and answered, "I haven't danced like that in forever." I sat mopping my brow like an old, fat grandma in an overheated church.

Penny laughed and said, "I don't dance at all!" I sipped that drink slower. I had really begun to feel the alcohol. I had not been drinking much since I'd moved back into the house with Barbara.

I took the drink from the bar and sat down at a table. It was cluttered with empties and an overflowing ashtray. The alcohol had caught up to me. All of a sudden, my past sneaked up and hammered me over the head. I could feel hot tears burning at my eyelids. Everything that had been bothering me seemed to wash over me in massive waves. Suddenly I was emotionally over-whelmed. I was ready to bolt and hide.

"Are you OK?" asked a concerned voice. It had a low, gentle timbre with a bit of a Midwestern twang. I looked up straight into the camera lady's eyes. They were very kind eyes, and the concern she was feeling was evident. I knew now why every-body talked to her. She really meant what she said; she was real. I noticed that she's wasn't as young as I had first thought. There were plenty of laugh lines and frown marks. Her temples were graying like a man's would. She had amber-colored highlights wrestling with the grey to cover the long, wavy, medium brown hair. I just sat there.

She picked up all the glasses and carried them to the bar, where Penny thanked her. They whispered for a minute. She returned for the ashtray and then brought me an empty one. I fig-ured she'd move on and continue cleaning. I wondered if maybe she worked there. But instead, she settled her feet wide like she was on the deck of a ship on the high seas, planted her hands on her hips, and asked, "Honey, are you OK?"

I glanced around. Where had everyone gone? I looked up into that kind face and began blurting out my worries about not being a millionaire anymore and how horrid it was waiting for *Dateline*. There was only a tiny change in her expression: a slightly cocked eyebrow. She gave a deep gurgle of laughter.

"Well, I can't help you with that, but I'd sure like to make sure you get home OK! Did you drive? You know, people who can't hold their water shouldn't drink so many of Penny's strong pours." She grinned away any hurt that message might have caused. She was politely telling me I was shitfaced.

"I'm not really drunk; I am just sad and tired. I can drive fine," I insisted.

"Famous last words," she snorted. "I'm going to close out, so wait here, don't move, and then I'll get you home. I can get you in the morning and bring you back to your car." She turned away and walked straight out the back door.

I must've misunderstood, because I went out the front door, climbed into my little car, and drove toward home with the intention of stopping for cigarettes on the way. Halfway home, I got out at a gas station, but its doors were locked. I really was wobbly on my pegs. When I turned around, I nearly fell over from fright. There was a cop car parked not a hundred feet from mine. I couldn't get caught tipsy. I would lose any credibility *Dateline* might give me if I got a DUI. On top of that, I would lose my commercial driver's license and be taken straight to jail.

I left my car right there at the pump and walked away down Dixie Highway. I didn't consider that there might be any objection to my abandoning the car at the pump. I crossed over to the west side of Dixie and walked up to the Walgreens drug store. It was closed too. Shit, I wanted a smoke. I turned around and headed back the way I'd come. I was cruising on foot down Dixie Highway past one in the morning, and I didn't much care.

I was startled when, all of a sudden, a minivan honked and whipped into the alleyway I was about to cross. And there was the camera lady, yelling out the window at me. "What in the world are you doing, walking on Dixie this late? I said I'd get you home! Where's your car? Don't you know people will think you're a hooker walking this strip?" She caught herself before I had a chance to respond, threw back her head, and let out a great bellow of laughter as she pushed the door open toward me. "Jesus, and now I'm gonna get arrested for picking up what they think is a hooker! Lord, have mercy!" She was giggling and gasping, wiping her streaming eyes as I plopped thankfully onto the seat. I didn't know if this was a good idea. I didn't know her at all, and I was pretty sure she'd just called me a hooker. I was really tipsy with all the alcohol running through my system.

She cackled again while trying to calm me down. "I'm April, by the way. Whew, haven't laughed like that in a while! What are you doing, walking down Dixie Highway in the middle of the night?" she asked through grinning lips.

"I was looking for cigarettes," I mumbled.

She turned in her seat and looked at me, saying, "We can handle that. Where exactly is your car? I know you left in one, you knucklehead. What's your name?"

"I'm Kathryn. I left it across the street at the gas station. It was closed, and a cop pulled in after I parked. I can't lose my CDL," I sighed. I was getting sleepy. She drove out of the alley and headed south on Dixie Highway.

"Why'd you run off? You know you are in no condition to drive, hence you strutting down the strip." She laughed again, mumbling about picking up hookers.

"You went out the back door, so I just assumed you didn't mean it," I said. My jaw cracked as I yawned.

"I always mean what I say, baby girl." I turned and looked at her. A look of complete sincerity, complemented by a friendly smile, lit up her face, and I felt safe. The skies had cleared over that tiny, wind-tossed boat, showing it to be unscathed and actually near shore. I heard April chuckling as I drifted off to sleep.

An extremely firm hand was shaking my arm and sloshing the alcohol around in my brain. I blearily opened my eyes and saw the camera lady. I sat bolt upright.

"Damn, you sleep soundly," she said, laughing. "Actually, you sleep just like my twelve-year-old son who wouldn't hear a cannon fire in his room."

"Is that your little Toyota?" she asked. We were back at the gas station.

"Yes," I said.

"Well, you were drunker than I thought. Whatever possessed you to leave it right at the pumps? Never mind! The same thing made you stroll down hooker highway." She was poking fun at me, and I wasn't sure I liked it, especially since she was right.

"There was a cop here," I stated.

"Well, there's an empty cop car. I think they park it there to deter speeders and thieves. How far do you live from here?" she asked.

"Less than a mile. So I'll be fine," I said.

"Yeah, those famous last words again. I'm going to follow behind you to see you get there safe. I take my mother-hen duties very seriously." She handed me a pack of Newports, saying, "I think these were what you were smoking." How strange it is to be with someone so observant? Most people only worry about themselves and what they can get.

"I'll pay you back, OK?" I offered. I don't do well with hand-outs. I'm used to being the giver.

"Man, don't worry about it. If it was gonna break the bank, I wouldn't have bought them." She waited for me to get out.

I climbed into my little car and drove home while she followed. When we arrived, I pulled into the tight driveway far enough so she could pull in behind. I parked and sat for a second, staring at the dark house. It looked lonely, since Barbara was out of town. It had been our home for more than a decade, and I'd soon be losing it. What a sad thought. I walked back to April's car, and she stuck her head out the window, saying, "I'll just wait until you get inside." She was going to say good-bye when she noticed my tears threatening. "Aw, what's the matter?"

"I had to file bankruptcy, and my house will be gone soon," I said. She didn't comment but just sat looking at me. I could see the wheels turning. I remembered her crack, made at The Bar, about people not drinking if they can't handle it. She probably thought I was nuts. I didn't want her to think that.

"Do you want to come in for a while?" I asked.

"Sure…but I can't stay long, since my dog has been home alone a long time already." She got out of the car, trying to squeeze by the prickly, brilliant pink bougainvillea hanging over the fence. I apologized as it snagged on her shirt. "No worries," she said.

We walked through the gate in the waist-high, dark brown privacy fence and on up the sidewalk that was crowded by knee-high weeds standing in for grass. She asked if I had a roommate, and I explained that she was out of town. I assured her that my furry ones were here, though. They tumbled out the door as soon as it opened. Draco, tall and blond, with his black-and-pink tongue lolling, plopped both front paws right on April's chest as Little One scrabbled her paws up the side of her leg. She laughed, saying, "Well, hello to you, too." She'd nearly been toppled off the front porch but held her ground. I yanked the dogs off. They say you can tell a good person by the way animals react to them. My fur-kids were confirming my suspicions.

We went into the house. I looked around at the evidence of the forthcoming bankruptcy. There wasn't a surface in the room that wasn't covered by a snowfall of white paper. My whole life seemed strewn about the room in piles of bills and invoices. I apologized for the mess, rearranged some papers so she could see the couch, and scooted off to the bathroom to get rid of about a gallon of processed alcohol.

When I got back, April was sitting comfortably squished between Draco, who was standing on the floor with his head leaning on her arm, and Little One draped along her leg like a brown-and-tan Chihuahua stole. I apologized for the mess and the dogs again.

"Really, no worries," she said, as she stroked the dogs. I reassigned space to more paperwork so I could sit too. We sat for a while in silence. She didn't seem in a hurry or inclined to fidget. It was very restful.

Eventually, I began to talk. April didn't react at all. It felt good talking about my childhood and my company and Haile. It all came tumbling out. I began to wonder if she was even listening. I'd never really met anyone who didn't interject with questions, interrupt with expressions of disbelief, or give unwanted advice. Most people don't have the patience to just listen. I figured she would likely be the same as everyone else. I was shocked when I realized it was nearly three thirty in the morning. I'd been talking for two hours straight. She asked if we could go out for a smoke.

She brushed off the dogs and followed me outside. She sat in a lawn chair and I sat on the steps. The dogs rustled around the yard. It was really dark out, because the moon had moved farther west, readying to set in preparation for sunrise. April nestled her chin in her hand, her arm propped on a knee, and stared down at her Skechers. She wore the big, black ones with the rocker-like bottoms. Her pants were baggy, black sweatpants made of something other than cotton or nylon. They were very slack in places, making me wonder if she'd lost some weight. She was still a big woman, but maybe she was trying to trim down.

"I thought I recognized you," she said. "I remember when that happened, which is weird, because I rarely watch the news, but I remember that you were on everywhere. I'm really sorry that happened to you." She sighed quietly, still looking at the ground. So, she had been listening. She began asking some very direct questions then, but without looking at me. It became very obvious to me that not only had she been listening, she had absorbed the vast majority of what I'd said. We talked more about the company and what was happening now. She asked when the *Dateline* segment was to air and if I was prepared for it if they were rough on me. She inquired about my mental health and asked if I should really be drinking, considering the medications I was on. I was flabbergasted. Nobody had ever paid attention to me the way she was, even the ones who were paid to listen — no, *especially* them. She wasn't telling me to suck it up and move on. She wasn't *telling* me anything. She only wanted to know how I was handling it all. I said that frankly, I wasn't. I was struggling mightily. When I began crying, she got up, threw away her cigarette butt, pulled me to my feet, and engulfed me in a big bear hug.

She held me while I cried and didn't shy away or try to make me stop. It made the tears flow even harder. Finally, I hiccoughed and coughed and realized I'd drenched her shirt with my tears and my drippy nose. I tried to wipe it all off, but she took my hand and said, "No worries. It'll dry, and it's washable." What a strange woman this was. She held onto my hand and asked me to look at her. I did.

"Is your stepfather still alive?" she asked.

"No, he died about two years after I ran away," I said.

She slung my hand down in anger and said, "Well, that's too fucking bad! I'd be getting on the road right now to go kill his ass!"

I laughed at her vehemence until I looked up, saw her expression, and remembered what she'd said earlier: "I always mean what I say, baby girl." It was a bit scary if she had meant it. She barely knew me.

By then, it was nearly five o'clock and the sky outside was brightening. April asked for my number as we went back inside. She put it in her phone and gave me hers, and apologized that she really had to go. Her dog would be thinking she'd fallen off the face of the earth. She promised to be in touch so we could get back together. I figured I had scared her, but good, and that she was just giving me the brush-off. Of course, it didn't sink in that she'd just spent the night listening to all my shit without running screaming from the house.

Fifteen minutes later, she called me. I recognized the laugh. "My dog LuLu has been peeing for the last three minutes," she said through the laughter.

"Oh, poor doggy," I said. "What kind is it?"

"She's a wimpy Rottweiler."

"Thanks for everything," I said.

"You're welcome. Let's do it again soon," she said. "Oh, and by the way, I have a fundraiser I'm shooting pics for on Monday at the Improv Comedy Club at City Place in West Palm. My friend Teri is playing there, too. Would you like to go? I can get another ticket."

"That'd be nice," I said.

"I'll call you, then." She hung up, and I wondered if she would really call. Talk about baggage! I could win the Bellhop Olympics with all of mine.

She called later in the day to see if I was hung over. I was, but didn't admit it. She gave me the time for Monday night and rang off right away, because she was at her son Vito's travel baseball game and couldn't talk because her son Vincent was mooching money off her for candy from the snack bar.

The next evening, she picked me up and we went to the Improv. I knew she was going to take pictures, but I didn't expect her to just take over the joint. She plopped me in a front-row table and took off. She was here, there, and everywhere, snapping pictures

143

of singles and groups, walking right up to crowded tables, rearranging everyone, laughing and joking. I would have been a nervous wreck. I can't even say hi to strangers unless they approach me first. I was impressed. As the room filled up, she eventually came and sat down with me. I'd already had a drink, sweet yet strong, and she ordered me another one when she ordered her scotch and soda. Whew, what a tough lady. She ordered dinner as well.

She leaned over the table to explain about the first act. It was to be her friend Teri Catlin. She is a musician who plays all original music that she writes completely by herself. She didn't describe Teri much and just left it at that.

A few minutes later, a stunning black woman hopped up on stage with loads of equipment. I didn't know if she was a roadie or the musician. She had butterscotch skin with brilliantly colored tattoos on her arms. Her hair was a trailing mass of dreadlocks. She had big eyes, thickly lashed, around pulsing green pupils. She was concentrating on setting up her amplifier and microphones when she looked up and saw April. The change in her face was electric. Her grimacing mouth blossomed into a dazzling smile.

"Hey my siSTAR, I didn't know you'd be here!" She bellowed. She scrambled to the edge of the stage to engulf April in a bone-crushing hug.

"Front and center, siSTAR! Where else would I be for the inimitable Teri Catlin?" April retorted.

Teri's face up close was a jumble of attributes. She had to be a mutt like me. She wasn't just black. Along with those startling green eyes that kind of looked blue, her skin was smooth, but her cheeks and nose were dusted with tiny, russet freckles. Her bone structure, while delicate, shouted strength and perseverance. She had a strong nose that didn't overtake her face. Her lips were full but not overwhelming, and her teeth were perfectly white and straight, like a dainty keyboard. April took her arm and turned her to me for an introduction. I had never thought much of tattoos and dreads, but on Teri, they were perfect.

"Are you gonna hang after your set?" April asked.

"Well, I wasn't planning to, but now you're here, I will if ya got a seat for me," she said.

"You know I got your back, my beautiful girl," April said, pointing to the chair next to her. Teri hurried back to the stage and was introduced to the crowd. She began singing, and I was mesmerized. I was shocked by how good she was. Some music was fun and some was inspirational. One song grabbed me to the depths of my soul and tore at my heart. It was called "American Girl." It was as if she had written it just for me. It talked about making a difference and about listening to the children to overcome our obstacles, that peace can conquer hate. It was wonderful.

I sat there thinking about that song and drinking my strong, sweet beverages. April was snapping pictures, so she wasn't paying attention to my mood swing. All of a sudden, I was shunted back to the days following Haile's death. I really cannot drink. It makes me too depressed. I just sat there, preoccupied, as Teri came off the stage and sat down. I was reliving my past as all of the comedians performed and, as everyone around me roared with laughter, I drank. I ate a teeny bit, but it wasn't enough to stave off the alcohol. I wasn't drunk yet, just extremely melancholy. As the show concluded, Teri and April were hooting over various jokes they thought stood out. As they left the table, I trailed behind, not caring particularly what came next.

We went to a bar next door to the Improv, and I ordered a frozen drink named Call-A-Cab. Thank God that April was driving. I laughed with all her friends and appeared to be having fun, while the entire time, the newsreels were playing in my head.

We left City Place and headed down to Clematis Street, where West Palm Beach goes to party. I don't even remember the name of the place we stopped at. I ordered 151-proof rum, and that was my undoing. I nearly yakked on the bar. April was now on red alert. She saw my face as I downed the shot and knew I was gonna lose it. She hoisted me up and hauled me into the bathroom, but I was too far gone to puke. My system was in revolt.

She took me out back to say we had to go. Missi, the bartender from The Bar Lake Worth, was there talking to Teri. April asked if I was OK, and I said yes. She propped me up at the table,

145

let me go, and down I went. Like a puppet with all its strings cut, I crashed to the ground. (In the days afterward, everybody told me all about it. Nobody was mean or nasty; they were just ribbing the new guy.)

April grabbed one side of my body and Missi got the other. Thank heaven they are both strong as oxen, because I am no lightweight. They carried me through the bar and out to April's van.

I heard April ask Missi, "Can you hold her while I get the door open?"

"Of course," Missi said, "you know how strong I am." I remember her panting in my ear as April let go of me. Poor Missi had more of a drunk on her hands than she could hold. I buckled in the middle and hit the ground hard.

April turned at the sound of my undignified "harrumph" as all the wind was knocked out of me.

"Oh, for fuck's sake, quit hitting the ground! You are gonna break something!" she bawled at me.

Then she started laughing, and Missi joined in. I didn't know what all the hilarity was about. The freaking ground hurt. April was hopping around like she was doing the pee-pee dance. They were having a jolly good time at my expense while I was splayed on the bricks. They poured me into the car, clipped me in with the seatbelt, and leaned the seat back. They smacked a kiss goodbye and Missi walked off. April stared at me before she shut the door. She had worry written all over her face.

"You'll stay with me tonight. I don't know what all you drank. I should have been paying better attention. I am sorry. If you get alcohol poisoning, I don't want you at home alone," she said. Talk about a guilt trip. I'm the one who overdid it, and April was doing the apologizing.

It hit me really hard that here was a veritable stranger who showed more care for me than some people I'd known my whole life. I began thinking that I should have cared for Haile, and that was when I fell apart. I started crying and apologizing to Haile in an anguished and determined way. April climbed behind the wheel and was completely at a loss. Nothing she could say was going to make it better. She started driving toward her home when my lamentations hit the hysterical point. She pulled over onto the edge of Interstate 95 and took my hands, trying to break through my grief. I couldn't stop. She calmly told me that she wouldn't drive with me in such bad shape, because it was too nerve-wracking. I just was not able to stop. She sat there until I geared down. I was still losing it, but at least she could safely drive us to her home.

When we got to her place, she left me strapped in the car until she had walked LuLu. Then they both escorted me inside. April put me in an old shirt to sleep in and put me to bed. It was, as it turned out, a very long night for her. I cried and wept and apologized nonstop for over four hours. She had nearly been driven to distraction by the time the sun came up. Nevertheless, she never chastised me or told me to suck it up. She just sat there with me, my head cradled in her lap, as I mourned.

All my baggage busted wide open that night. April didn't push me away or disparage me. I will be eternally grateful for that night, because I finally realized how unselfish a true friend could be. She held the pot while I puked; she kept a cool, wet rag on my head; she didn't cry and tell me my feelings were too much to handle; she wasn't mad from missing sleep. I'd never experienced that before with anybody. It was very therapeutic.

9. Waiting for Dateline

I won't insult your intelligence by saying that I was cured after that night. That is far from the case; however, there is something intrinsically medicinal about knowing someone has your back. Ever since my mom turned to defend Butch instead of me, I have felt too unworthy to expect anyone's support. April wasn't exactly letting me be my typical standoffish self. She bullied her way into the position of chief protector and confidante, and I don't think a grenade could have budged her from her stance as my friend. As I said before, she is a very unusual woman.

We got together a few times over the next week. She was hungry to learn about my past demons. She wanted me to bring every dark secret into the light so she could dissect them. She said she'd never met anyone who'd been sexually abused as a child, at least none she was aware of. It bordered on a morbid curiosity and was beginning to concern me until she changed the focus and started delving into my treatment. She said that she didn't think the counseling I'd had since Haile was helping nearly enough. She didn't feel that my relating all the tales of anguish to her the night she'd been such a good listener was normal. She said I was trapped in the past, and then she changed the subject. For the moment, she had asked enough, and I could see that wheels were spinning behind her eyes.

On that Sunday, she called to say that Teri Catlin had invited her to a modern dance studio called Groovolution for an anniversary party that evening. She invited me, saying she couldn't wait for me to get to know Teri. There was abuse in Teri's background, she had also been homeless, and April thought that since Teri and I had these things in common, we might really relate well to each other.

We drove together and met Teri inside the studio. Teri giggled with me a bit about the last time we'd met, adding that she didn't have much room to talk, because she'd been pretty bad herself.

The show was really fun to watch. A good portion of it was performed under black lights, and the dancers were painted and adorned in startling fluorescent colors. For me it was a really good distraction. After the show, the three of us hung around in the parking lot. We'd made a beer run and sat drinking and talking about life. Teri admitted to me that she was glad we had met again and now understood my morose mood the night at the Improv Comedy Club. She said I'd scared her because of my lack of response to the sketches. We laughed at my foibles and began talking about her experiences as a runaway in Flint, Michigan. You had to be one tough mother to survive the streets of Flint at any time in the last thirty years. The FBI ranks it as the single most violent place in America. It has held this distinction for years, she explained. She had lived on its violent streets from the tender age of fourteen.

The three of us really connected that night. April, despite a very vanilla upbringing, has tremendous empathy in her being. She feels the emotions of those she cares for completely. She told Teri and me how happy she was that we were getting acquainted, since she loves us both and wants the best for us. How much better can life get than when you have good friends to share it with?

I asked Teri if she could play "American Girl" for me, the song I had liked so much from the other night. She balked a bit until I was prepared to get on my knees and beg. She still made me haggle, but eventually, she broke out her guitar, climbed on the hood of her SUV, and began to serenade us. It was amazing. She had sung just four songs at the Improv. Tonight she entertained us with many more. The three of us sang boisterously, two of us completely out of tune but with lots of gusto. April knows just about every word to every one of Teri's songs. She says they sing straight to her soul, making her whole heart smile.

Then Teri cranked up the demo for her new CD on the SUV's stereo. I parked myself in the driver's seat and listened to "American Girl" over and over. The time flew by until April insisted she was too old to be spending the night in a parking lot. So she pried me and Teri apart, kissed Teri good-bye and hustled my tipsy butt into the car. I sat wailing "American Girl" for the next twenty minutes until April cried foul. She should've kept her mouth shut, because when I fell quiet, I disappeared into hell. Alcohol seems to turn a key that opens my emotional strongbox. Consciously, I get lost in a morass of guilt about Haile, and subconsciously, about my own childhood. I began crying and apologizing again to Haile.

April drove us along in stoic silence. She let my sniveling continue until I needed air. Then she informed me that I simply should not drink. She suggested that I needed to learn to unleash my emotions while sober to enable me to react to them better and face them head-on, that I needed clarity to harness my defenses against all the pain. She got all that out just in time for me to begin wailing again. I didn't immediately react to those kernels of advice, but my subconscious did. Deep down, I knew I had to start addressing my issues. April took care of me again that night and just let me cry it out without any judgment.

The next day, she handed me a journal and suggested I begin writing down my feelings. She wanted me to start with my childhood and not with Haile and the closing of the schools. She said it might help even out my burdens to put them on paper. She didn't push, exactly, but it was clear that this wasn't just a simple request. She'd spent some terrible nights with me, and this was how I could do something to show her I wanted to get better.

That evening, I was fretful about writing, because I knew it would suck. So instead of doing that, I put in a call to Robbie

Gordon, the *Dateline* producer. I was more panicky about not hearing from *Dateline* than I was about writing about my past.

The very next day, I got the call I had been waiting for. I was on a StairMaster machine in the FAU gymnasium when Robbie called back. My chest was heaving, my heart was pounding, and my phone was soon drenched with sweat dripping down off my ear. Robbie was very astute, and, hearing my heavy breathing, wanted to know if I was OK. I laughed a slightly nervous laugh and explained what I was doing when she called.

She apologized for the delay in the piece that was to include me. She said the lawyers from NBC and the state of Florida had been haggling over the portion of the story regarding the bus inspection on the day Haile died. They'd finally decided to drop that part from the segment. So I'd only be throwing the state under one side of the bus. Just the faulty background checks were to be kept in. Not that it really mattered much now, since Katie's Kids Learning Center, Inc. had been closed down for good. They couldn't chastise me anymore.

She told me that the story on *Dateline* would be airing at ten o'clock that Friday across the country on the NBC Television Network. That week's show would be split into six segments investigating pre-schools that harbored employees with criminal backgrounds. That made me nervous, because I'd unknowingly had people working for me who had criminal backgrounds, never mind that the state had given them a clean background check. I really hoped I was going to come out looking acceptable. Then Robbie had to rush off the phone, so we said good-bye and hung up.

I stood there in the middle of the gym, dripping sweat and ramping up to a panic attack. I had been waiting so long for this. What if I appeared in a bad light? I could never handle that. I called Barbara to warn her that the story was going to air on Friday night. She was not pleased. Our lives were such hell those long months while news crews hunted me down everywhere. She couldn't be involved with the madness because she worked for the school district. We couldn't take the chance of her losing her job. I told her I would stay somewhere else for a while until it all passed over.

I called April, and she was ecstatic for me. She had become such a godsend. I had never felt so emotionally supported in my life. She immediately offered to help with whatever I needed. I didn't want to ask if I could stay with her. I had been quit a burden already.

The third person I called was Katie LaGrone, who is one of the nicest people you'd ever want to meet. She's an investigative reporter for WPTV Channel 5, the NBC affiliate in Palm Beach County. She had always been very fair with me. As I mentioned many chapters ago, Katie used to tease me that I was more famous than she was, and I'd assure her that I was just more infamous. I asked what her opinion was on my part of the *Dateline* piece, saying that I was very nervous about it. She thought I would come off fine. She said it was opportune that I had called, because she had been about to call me. She wanted to do a lead-in piece on the five-o'clock news. They would use it as a teaser, tantalizing viewers to watch *Dateline* later that night.

The sweating got worse, but the panic attack had subsided. Katie wanted me to meet her at the WPTV studios to do the interview in two days. This was going to be tough. I had put on a few pounds, had no nice clothes to wear, no money to buy any, and I needed good makeup to wear for the camera. I'd look terrible otherwise. What a truly female situation! Barbara was earning a salary, but she'd just told me she wanted no part of any of this. I couldn't ask her for help. I decided that I couldn't worry about it. I just didn't have the money.

My workout was ruined by then, and the exercise high was long gone. I was terrified of the imminent future; the "what-ifs" returned in full force. Just then, April called to see how I was doing. We seemed to be telepathically connected. She knew I'd be worried. I told her all my woes as I drove to pick up Barbara from work—we were down to one car now. I told April what Barbara had said, and she told me not to worry. She talked to me until I got to Barbara's school, outlining what I needed to do before Thursday when I'd meet up with Katie LaGrone. On the way home, Barbara told me that she needed the car for the rest of the week, because she had to go to out-of-town meetings. I called

April when I got home and explained that I no longer had the use of a car. She told me to pack some clothes and that I should come and stay at her house. She offered to chauffeur me around the rest of the week. I got all choked up. I knew she meant it. I hated asking for help, to impose, but when I thought about it, I realized I hadn't asked for help. April had offered. That's a big difference for someone who has always been on the giving end of things.

April picked me up at my house that afternoon. We dropped off my stuff at her little house in nearby Lantana and headed back out to the car.

"Where are we going?" I asked.

"Wherever you need to go for clothes and makeup," she said, and then laughed, adding, "I'm a Walmart kind of gal, if you hadn't noticed, and I don't think that'll do for this situation."

I dug in my heels and said, "I don't have the money to go." She looked at me like I'd just fallen out of the clouds.

"Well, no shit, Sherlock! You already told me that," she said.

"Then where are we going?"

She rolled her eyes heavenward, and I could see her lips counting to ten. I had to laugh. She looked pissed and pious all at the same time.

"Get in the van and tell me where you want to go. And no more stupid questions!"

I really didn't want to. I had never taken handouts! I learned that very young from my dad's family. You do it on your own or not at all. She watched my face as I wrestled with myself.

"Listen to me," she said. "No more shenanigans. Get your ass in that van before I throw you in there." I remembered her 'I mean what I say' comment and scurried into the van. I could fight better from the comfort of my seat. I do not remember anyone ever just putting me in my place like that—not in recent memory, anyway. I'd been the boss so long that I was not exactly comfortable with someone taking over. "Look," she said, "let's get something straight. I am not giving you a handout."

Damn, she's hit the nail on the head, I thought.

"I have some ideas about the future, and I intend to get back any investment I make in you now by a hundredfold," she went on.

Those words got my attention. Then she just shut me down, saying we'd talk about it later. I turned and looked at her. She had a very stubborn set to her jaw. So I left it alone. Boy, was I changing.

I told her we should go to Boca Towne Center in Boca Raton, a few miles to the south. That's where I had bought makeup for the *Dateline* interview. I warned April that it'd be expensive, and I got a harrumph in response. So I held my peace and turned up the radio.

Usually I hate shopping; it is sheer boredom for someone of my temperament, combined with ADHD. I soon learned that April hated shopping even more than I did. We walked into the makeup place, and she told the girl I had an interview on the news in a couple of days and to set me up. The girl started to make suggestions, and April just held up her hand. She said we were in a hurry and told the attendant to just give me whatever I needed to look good in high definition. The girl's jaw dropped. We were in a MAC store, which is a bit on the pricey side, and the makeup artist probably didn't get many requests for just "everything." She sat me in a chair and went to work, explaining how to apply all the products. I enjoyed it but noticed that there were plenty of sighs and some grumbling over in the peanut gallery.

When I peered into the mirror, I could hardly believe the transformation in my appearance. I had been too out of it the last time I was made up to go on camera to appreciate how nice I had looked. It felt great. I looked at April with appreciation glimmering in my eyes along with some tears of thanks.

"If you think you get to sit there and do all that again because you cry the stuff off, then think again," she said, smiling to help take the sting out of her remark. The girl started itemizing all the products again when April told her just to ring it up and to add all the brushy things and something to carry it all in. I could see the dollar signs twirling in the girl's eyes as she considered her commission. The bill was astronomical, but April didn't even blink. She handed over her American Express Gold Card, and I'm pretty sure that she never really looked at the total. Man, that was weird. I had been worth millions but never spent anything on myself, and then here was this woman, my new friend, picking up the tab for me. I had to wonder if I was back in the Twilight Zone.

I shook my head as we headed toward the Loft, a clothing store, where everything unfolded in the same way as at MAC. April told the salesgirl to figure out my size and find what I wanted, and to hurry up about it. She grinned again, but I knew she meant it. I just walked along, feeling for the softest things that attracted me. I love soft clothes. The girl carried my choices to the dressing room and left me there. About five minutes later, there was a tap on the door and several other things were handed to me through the crack when I opened it. These were items that I would not have picked for myself, and I said so. The clerk said April had picked them out. (How'd she know her name?) God, April could be bossy and opinionated, but she also turned out to be right. Colors I never would have chosen for myself looked excellent with my skin tone. For someone who shopped at Walmart, she had excellent taste.

I came wagging all the goodies out of the dressing room and asked which I should get. She asked if they all fit, and I said yes. She took the whole bundle from me and plopped it on the counter. Then she told the girl to see what else I needed and to get pastel colors. The same thing happened at the checkout. She just paid, no questions asked. For every two hundred and fifty bucks we spent, we received a coupon for twenty-five dollars off any future fifty-dollar purchase. I walked out the door with seven coupons. April said we could come back when they were good. I was blown away.

The last stop was Victoria's Secret. I have never owned so many panties in my life! Shopping is fun when you aren't agonizing over everything. I decided that if I was ever successful again, this was how I wanted to shop.

April looked smug. She'd won, and she knew it. She had broken down one of my biggest barriers, and she knew I was happy for it.

On the way home, I called the PR firm to let them know about the interview coming up and said that I needed a refresher course on what questions to avoid. I had given them a fifteen-thousand-dollar retainer back when I still had money, which we were to use to promote my name once *Dateline* aired. They said to come in before my interview. April was confused about the PR firm, and I explained.

Tonya called and told me she was coming down the next day so she could be there for me during the *Dateline* broadcast on Friday. I balked a bit. Here I was, staying at April's, and I couldn't very well just invite someone else. But I should've known she'd be watching me when I looked over at her. It is eerie how April sort of reads my mind. She told me Tonya was welcome at the house also.

Tonya and April got on together like two peas in a pod. They are both quite a bit older than I am, and together they tended to hover around me like a pair of mother hens, clucking away.

Tonya had just had surgery on her leg and was hobbled a bit by a brace and a cane. That didn't stop her from proverbially kicking my ass over my depression. She said everything would work out for the best and to begin thinking positively. She speaks in a molasses tempo and can be mistaken for being a bit slow on the uptake. However, if you stop rushing around and listen to her, you realize how measured her words are and how intelligent she is. She doesn't just blurt out things; she structures her thoughts before she speaks. With my ADHD, I find her hard to follow at times, but April understood her easily.

On that Thursday morning, we drove to the offices of Transmedia, the PR firm, to meet with Tom Madden, the owner. I was as nervous as a long-tailed cat slinking through a room full of rocking chairs. It had been a long time since I had been prepped for an interview. Besides, even though I felt Katie LaGrone would be fair, I couldn't bank on her bosses not wanting her to go in for the kill.

We sat in a conference room, Tonya and April flanking me like a pair of sentries guarding priceless jewelry. I looked up and noticed a beautiful, wood-mounted photo on the wall. It was a plaque commemorating the thousand trees I had planted in Haile's name through the organization Seed Our Future. I had wanted to create a scholarship in her name at FAU but had run into too much legal red tape.

The picture on the plaque is of a soothing green hillside dotted with trees, a backdrop to the lone tree in the foreground. The caption reads: *In loving memory of Haile Brockington, who died Aug. 5, 2010, I plant these 1,000 trees in a deforested area of the world in hopes this tragedy may lead to many positive changes in the pre-school industry that will keep children like Haile safe and make the air they breathe and the planet on which they play more life-supporting.* I got a bit tense from the memory, and April zeroed in on my stiffening posture. Her gaze followed mine to the plaque. Her eyes shimmered with tears as she read it. I was amazed by how involved she already was with the situation. She blinked at me and smiled to show her understanding as Tom Madden walked in with two assistants.

We talked trivialities for a bit. We weren't there nearly as long as the last time, perhaps a half hour. We discussed my wardrobe and hair. That way, Tom thought, NBC's WPTV Channel 5 would portray me as a sympathetic individual and not as a monster.

We talked about opportunities for me to use my experiences to help stop similar tragedies. My PR people were very supportive, but not much help, really. I was a bit confused by their lack of inventiveness. I needed help to get my name out there so I could position myself to do advocacy as well as find financial opportunities. That was what I was paying them for. When I brought up a potential book idea, they were rather mute, just as they were when I said maybe I could represent an alarm company. They breezed by all that and concluded the meeting. Their only suggestion was to hook up my name with an online background check company, but said that there probably wouldn't be money in it for me. I felt disappointed and asked them to keep looking.

April and Tonya were both concerned about the meeting. They wanted more from the company for me because of what I'd paid them. I was torn because I have this hitch in my personality that makes me feel I have to pay those close to me to stick around. I'd done it repeatedly in the past with gifts of vans to my staff and diamond jewelry to friends, cars for my siblings, and thousands of dollars over the years for my mom. I had never felt like anyone would be with me just for me. In a sense, I bribed them so that I'd not be alone. I hadn't been aware of this habit, but April told me about it loud and clear, repeatedly. She said I needed to find people who liked me without expectations of largesse. She probably is the first one to ever give to me instead of the reverse, and it was confusing. I just never felt worthy without paying for things myself.

We stopped for a quick lunch before my interview. April and Tonya chatted and ate while I sat and stared in silence. Anything passing my lips would have come right back out.

There was silence in the car as we drove to the television studios, and then as the three of us sat in a fog of cigarette smoke in the parking lot. I was truly worried about the ensuing interview. I didn't know whether to be calmly happy that things were for the best or to admit that I was dead. My confused feelings were like what you might feel attending a funeral when you aren't sure if it's yours or not.

We walked into the airy, two-story lobby and approached the receptionist. She told us that Katie was out and that her calendar indicated that we had arrived an hour early. April, snorting under her breath, said, "That's great! Now we get to wait longer for the guillotine to fall." We filed back out to the car like a condemned trio headed for the tumbril cart. Everyone lit up again and watched the smoke dissipate into the hot March afternoon. I was climbing the walls, because to me, it felt like the clock was ticking backwards.

We talked quietly about what the interview should be like and its potential effect upon my future. April and Tonya tried to be positive for me, but I kept reminding myself that it was my head on the block.

When the hour had passed, we returned to the station lobby where the receptionist informed us that Katie would be right with us. We sat on the leather couches, and April patted my knee in support. She sighed loudly and crossed her arms over her chest. I think she was as nervous for me as I was.

When Katie finally arrived, I could literally feel April relax. How could you be scared of a little pixie dressed like a particularly impish pirate? Katie is petite and willowy. She was sporting a striped blouse and black pants with gold hoop earrings. Her long, brown hair swirled around her shoulders as I introduced her to my friends. Her welcome to me was genuinely warm, as were her questions about my welfare.

She took us outside to do the interview and explained why she was hefting all the camera equipment: her cameraman's wife had just given birth and he was on leave. She sat me down at a picnic table and began setting up the tripod. She made a joke about wishing one of us were a photographer. She wanted help framing the shot effectively. I pointed out that April is a photo pro. She grinned and turned to April with a pleading expression.

"Would you have a look for me, please?" Katie asked April.

"Sure, I can do that," April said. "I would not recommend that swaying palm tree casting shadows behind Kathryn's head; it will be too distracting." I repositioned myself while I baked in the hot south Florida sun. Katie moved the camera and April stepped behind her.

She took a look and said, "Absolutely not."

"Why?" asked Katie.

"We can't have her looking like a jailbird!"

Everyone turned to look behind me. There was a huge, black wrought-iron fence in the background.

"That would definitely send the wrong message," Tonya said. We all looked at one another and burst out laughing. Thankfully, some of the tension was broken, and I even managed a smile. April stood me up and asked Tonya to help her move the picnic table. They placed it where April thought it would look best and sat me down again. I was so hot in the direct sun that I could feel the sweat popping out all over my body. If we didn't hurry, I was sure I would melt and so would all of my expensive makeup.

Katie was very thorough about the past: details regarding Haile, the bad background checks, closing the schools, my financial collapse, and strategies for the future were all reviewed. When we finished, I felt much calmer, but when I stood up, my shirt was plastered to my back. The outline of my iPad was marked with sweat on my pants, and I felt like I had a case of heat stroke.

We did a few takes of us walking together and of Katie looking at me, then wrapped it up.

"Excuse me," said April. "Kathryn, why don't you show Katie what you have been holding and looking at this whole time?"

"What have you got there?" Katie asked. I could feel all my emotions surge to the surface, and it took a moment to respond. I could feel the sweat rolling down my back, but then I composed myself.

"It's a picture of Haile," I said. "I keep it with me so I will never forget. It helps me focus on what I want to do in the future to stop this from happening again."

"Just a minute," Katie said. She pulled the camera back out and shot some footage over my shoulder showing Haile's picture and me together. She asked me to explain why I had it and how it helped me.

"That was amazing," she said. "It really ties in your emotional investment with your desire to fix things."

We chatted for a few minutes about her young son and his issues with pre-school. He'd fallen and gashed his forehead. We agreed that even with the best staff, accidents could happen; some accidents were just much worse than others. We said goodbye and she asked me to keep in touch, especially if I did write a book. She wanted to read it.

April put her arm around me as we walked to the car. Tonya gave me a big hug before we got in. It had been a very emotional day so far, and they wanted to show they were there for me. I heaved huge sighs of relief.

"I think that was incredible," April said. "I cannot imagine them being able to do anything with that piece other than to portray you as very sympathetic and determined to fix the problem."

"If the *Dateline* piece is as good, you will be vindicated fully," Tonya said.

"I am still worried," I said. They both looked at me and held their peace.

We went back to April's house, and the three of us passed out for a few hours. What an emotional roller coaster the last year and a half had been. Now there was a chance of some closure. I sure hoped that would happen. We all trooped to The Bar Lake Worth that night, and I was entertained by the karaoke singers and soothed by the alcohol. We got home well after two in the morning. For once, the alcohol didn't induce remorse.

April and Tonya went to sleep quickly, but I lay in bed wringing my hands and reviewing the past. Memories swirled together in a vortex of feelings. I was still very disappointed with my mother for choosing Butch over me. I was furious with Petra and Amanda for letting Haile die. I was terrified about being broke. I was anxious about Barbara leaving and being alone. Nevertheless, I was so happy I had met April. She had been keeping me sane. I didn't sleep a wink until I broke down and took my Xanax and Trazodone. I was fearful about the true outcome of the interviews. I slept soundly until well past noon the next day. With those drugs in me, I wouldn't have been roused any earlier, even if a trumpet had been blasting notes into my ear.

April had spent the evening before looking for a place to watch the interviews, because she didn't have a TV. We had a few options for the ten-o'clock *Dateline* show, but we only had The Bar for the five-o'clock newscast. I sat around dozily, trying to fight off the aftereffects of the drugs. I really didn't care where we watched the shows. I was super depressed, even though I thought things would be OK. I couldn't get excited after being made to wait so long.

I heard April on the phone talking to someone about watching *Dateline* with us. I got curious. I knew Penny and Missi would be working at The Bar and that Julie had her daughter. I'm sure April had other friends, but I didn't think I knew any of them well enough to share this time with.

When she got off the phone, she was all smiles. She sat down next to me on the porch and lit a grape Swisher Sweets cigar.

I was looking at her and waiting for her to spill the news as she sat there, slowly exhaling.

"Well?" I asked.

"Teri has rearranged her schedule so she can be with us," she said.

"Did she really? That is so amazing. I like her and would love for her to come up here for it," I said. Teri is a very busy musician and it was a Friday night. It made me feel great that she would come all the way up from Fort Lauderdale to be with me for moral support.

April, Tonya, and I rolled up to The Bar at four forty-five that Friday afternoon. The sun scorched the windshield as we waited for Teri. Without sunglasses, the glare was so bright for my eyes that I shut them against the painful, brilliant intrusion. I thought about how these interviews could shine some much-needed illumination into my dark frame of mind. Maybe they could be as essential to my life as the brilliant sunlight was to the earth.

Teri cruised in a few minutes later. We all hugged, and I introduced Teri and Tonya to each other. We talked for a moment about how the WPTV interview had gone until April insisted we move inside. She wiped off the sweat dripping into her eyes and complained she'd melt into a huge grease spot if we didn't find air conditioning, *stat*. What a hot winter it had been. We hoped it didn't foreshadow a miserable summer wracked by hurricanes. Some say that the best thing about south Florida is indoor climate control.

Walking into The Bar at this time of day was a new experience for me. The only time I had ever been in any bar was at night. The humidity and heat were so miserable outside, but in the bar it was as cold and dark as a tomb. It was a major transition for my eyes. I almost bumped into the wall. The darkness inside seemed to envelop me like my miserable thoughts did.

I remember feeling my way to the bar, laying my backpack down, and ordering a drink. I began to sit down. Then panic struck, and I didn't know if I had to pee, puke, or poop. I rushed to the bathroom. It was a false alarm, but I felt like I was starting to lose it. I needed to try to calm myself down. I splashed some water on my face. I looked in the mirror and into my eyes, repeatedly telling myself that I was all right.

All the waiting had come down to this. I was holed up in a tiny restroom in a little local bar, waiting to learn my fate. I know it sounds ridiculous, but the news could have ruined the rest of my life if I were made out to be a monster. All I had ever wanted to do was to help children. I just had to settle down and wait to see what would happen.

I walked back to the bar, plopped myself onto the stool, and drank my first drink down with barely a pause to take air. I about gagged as my mouth puckered up. The daytime bartender, Alex, didn't have a way with a Grape Nerd. It was so tart that I couldn't help smacking my lips to release the saliva glands from flood mode. Teri ordered a heavy Irish Guinness beer, Tonya ordered a Grape Nerd, and April abstained. She knew she was in for a long night, no matter how the interviews turned out. I was an emotional wreck, and the alcohol wasn't likely to help.

I asked Alex for another drink. The pep talk I had had with myself in the mirror moments ago wasn't working. I needed something to calm me down. I asked Alex to make this one with a little less pucker. He laughed and apologized for not knowing the correct mix, explaining that his customers were more beer-and-whiskey type folks. I guzzled my second one as soon as I took the glass from his hand. Alex stood there with eyebrows raised and asked if I'd like another. The answer was yes.

Tonya was trying to engage me in small talk, but it was not helping at all. I was too distracted and was becoming irritated, because what I really wanted was to be left alone. I was too anxious to chat. Of course, Tonya didn't know that, and I didn't mean to be rude, but I ignored her anyway. April left me to myself and kept herself occupied talking with Teri.

When we had been looking for somewhere to watch the news, April had asked Penny (who, as it turned out, owned The Bar) if we could watch the five-o'clock news there. She had agreed and offered to tell Alex that we'd need quiet when the broadcast came on. When the news began, there was a teaser to promo my story. I went wild calling for the juke box to be shut off and for people to be quiet so I could hear. Everyone at the bar stared at me with their jaws dropped, including my friends.

I made a mad dash for the toilet. I was panicking and my stomach was heaving. I couldn't miss the news, so in an attempt to clear my stomach I shoved my fingers down my throat but didn't throw up. My head was spinning as I splashed more water on my face, washed my hands, and headed back to the bar. April watched me closely as I approached, concern written all over her face. She asked if I was OK and let me be when I said yes.

I watched every commercial while white-knuckling the bar rail. The announcer reminded us of the upcoming piece at every break, and it drove me crazy. Everyone else was enjoying the music and their friends, while I was losing my mind. Why couldn't they just show the clip already? I was so impatient.

Alex had turned the TV volume up and down so many times that he finally released the remote into my custody. He was working, after all. After the fourth or fifth time I asked that the juke box volume be lowered, the other patrons caught on that I was overwrought and let Alex turn it off until the news was over. Everyone was curious by now to know what my deal was. They had all nodded and acknowledged April, but they didn't know me at all. I am sure they were a bit afraid of the crazy black chick wielding the remote like a sword, turning green and heading for the toilet every few minutes. I just needed to feel better, and if puking helped, then so be it. Being calm was out of the question.

I tried to be patient, but wanted to yell at the screen as if it would speed up the newscast. My heart was racing so fast, you'd almost think that I was headed for a coronary, and my breathing fluctuated so much that I thought I'd pass out. April finally switched seats with Tonya and took my hand, squeezed it hard, and held it in her lap. I nearly burst into tears. Her human touch calmed me and regulated my system, and I felt better.

By five forty, April had the four of us huddled together in the smoky atmosphere, whispering about potential benefits of being on the news. They were trying to distract me. And then we almost missed it! By the time the item came on, I was emotionally drained and well on my way to being drunk. Everyone kept swiveling their heads between the newscast and me. You'd have thought they were watching a tennis match. Now everyone understood why the crazy chick was so hyper.

April's backdrop for the interview was perfect. I looked sincere and determined to fight for change. My true emotions shone through. There wasn't a dry eye in the place when Katie told of how I carried Haile's picture everywhere with me so I would never forget. It was brilliant. I was shown to be blameless. It was true vindication. This time, I was breathless from joy! There was no way *Dateline* could turn me into a monster after that, could they?

I was so relieved when Katie LaGrone signed off. My friends hugged and kissed me and pounded my back like some conquering hero. One woman came over to me and gave me a big hug. She was happy that I was raising the issue of people being left behind in vans. The woman told me that her mother had been forgotten in a van at a nursing home and had died because of it. I thanked her and told her I was sorry for her loss.

I wanted to stay excited, but there was the big *Dateline* interview coming later that night. No, I couldn't be satisfied that the local news story went well, I still had to stress about the other one. I'm nuts that way. It was only six o'clock. I still had four hours of doubt to endure before the *Dateline* program would air. Four hours seemed like four years.

April suggested we go to The Cottage down on Lucerne Avenue in Lake Worth to get something to eat. Teri chimed in to say it was one of her favorite places, but I didn't feel hungry. If I did eat, I thought I would likely have to throw up, but I was glad we were going somewhere. And I would try to think about something else. I didn't believe it was going to work, but I was sure going to try. I studied my friends, old and new, as we paid our tabs. They may never know how glad I was that they were beside me, giving me their support. I thanked Alex for letting me handle the remote, and we left.

We arrived at The Cottage as the sun was just about to set. The temperature had dropped. It wasn't as hot as earlier. We decided to eat outside, because it truly was a beautiful, balmy night.

Everyone put in their orders. All I wanted was another drink. I was afraid that if I put any food in my stomach, I mightn't be able to keep it down. I ignored the prospect that a lot of alcohol would likely have the same effect. When the food came, I struggled to stay in the moment. I did not want to disappear into my past after the triumph on the local news. It was hard and always had been. I was more aware of not staying in the moment now that April was helping me to recognize the signs and to fight them off. Nevertheless, I don't remember eating or drinking or talking. I was just there.

We finished dinner and went to the grocery store to get beer and wine coolers. I stayed in Teri's car and listened to her song, "American Girl." I don't think a song has ever affected me the way that one does. My friends returned, and together we headed to the home of Lorinda, my tutor and friend from FAU, to watch *Dateline*. Her mother and sisters had prepared appetizers for us, but no one was very hungry. I felt bad that they had gone to all that trouble, especially since April, Tonya, and Teri were all stuffed. Eating was not an option for me.

I was really nervous. At ten o'clock, *Dateline* finally started, but we still had a wait, because our story was slated to be the second-to-last of the six segments scheduled. The stories centered on pre-school facilities whose owners had criminal backgrounds (and on me, who did not). They had all been approved for licenses by their various states, and the parents had been clueless.

The first segment began. It was about a couple whose child died because the owner of his pre-school taped his mouth shut by wrapping duct tape around his head. She then taped his hands together because he would not settle down and be quiet for a nap. As I remember, the owner had a criminal record for child abuse. I felt wretched for the death of that child and for the parents who lost him. It was a wrenching story, and I could hardly watch the other segments. Everyone was mesmerized by the stories. They were tragic and bordered on the unbelievable.

One state boasted that it had the highest standards in the country when it came to screening owner applications for pre-schools. Robbie Gordon and Chris Hansen had to prove that this claim was just wrong, and they succeeded. *Dateline*'s undercover researchers hunted up three of the most heinous criminals they could find who met their criteria, and, posing as these offenders, they filed for licensure in that particular state. The state had put the names of the three through their "tough" screening process, and guess what happened? The three criminals were approved and cleared as responsible citizens who could be entrusted to operate pre-schools.

I felt bad for that state's spokesperson when this bombshell was dropped on her. She and Chris Hansen were standing in a courtroom, where he explained what they had been after, and she repeated how good they were at background screening. I thought she'd faint when he showed her who the real "applicants" were. The shock of his next bombshell nearly wiped her out. Not only were the applicants criminals, they were so bad that all three had been executed for their crimes. Her comment that the state might need more work on its background check procedures sent April into uncontrollable laughter. It was just so unbelievable.

After a commercial break, the next segment came on. I knew that this wasn't going to be a good interview. They were tearing everyone to shreds. I couldn't sit still and was up and down and heading outside for a smoke. By the third and fourth segment, I started drinking shots, trembling and running out to smoke more. By the time my segment was to come on, I wasn't sure I would be able to watch. April came out to smoke and to tell me I was up next. Chris had interviewed me for over an hour so many months earlier that on that long-awaited Friday night, I could not remember one thing he had asked me.

Back inside, April sat next to me on the couch, holding my hands in one large mitt. I was cold from fright, and she was chafing warmth into my limbs with her other hand. Her hands are very strong, and I was distracted by them as my interview began. I was a bit tipsy by then, and what struck me most was that I looked very professional on TV despite how sad I had been on that day. I appeared calm and poised. The memories of our hour-long interview rushed back to me, and all of a sudden I knew I was going to be OK. I really was a gem in a pile of rocks. Yes,

Haile had died, but they were telling the world that her death was not my fault. If only my subconscious had been paying attention. I was relieved but still extremely emotional.

That segment about Haile and me may only have been about five minutes long, but I had been vindicated on national television. When the *Dateline* piece was finally over, I was glad. With my emotions both high and low, I felt like I was on a roller coaster that would never end. Everyone was talking at once, it seemed. They were all saying the same thing: that I was amazing.

April left me while she ran to her house to get something. I stayed in Teri's SUV, wailing along to "American Girl" when April returned. She presented me with an inspirational book. It was a gift to commemorate my surviving *Dateline*. I was so happy she was in my life and that she had given me Teri, too. What a true friend. I was so pleased about the way the day had ended.

That night, I slept like a baby. The alcohol was still in my system, and it helped me to crash. I slept for about twelve hours. When I awoke, I had a major hangover, but with a head clear enough to give thought to what I was going to do when I grew up. I lay in bed with relief, but still, angst was wrestling for top position in my troubled mind. The interviews had turned out better than in my wildest dreams, yet I had no immediate purpose in my life.

I was glad the *Dateline* piece was over. But what was I to do now? I was thankful it had aired in March, because if the interview had come out sooner, I probably wouldn't have finished my bachelor's degree. I would have started looking for a job, hoping to do more advocacy work or anything worthwhile to make me once again a productive and contributing member of society.

I lay there thinking about the night before. I had had quite a lot to drink. I recalled April telling me that she had some ideas for the future. One idea oozed through the remaining haze of the effects of alcohol and took seed in my always-worried brain. April wanted us to create an alarm system that was superior to anything on the market for ensuring child safety. The idea germinated and took root. Here was something to be excited about.

I had learned in our short acquaintance that whatever April said, she meant. Despite that, I was still having a hard time believing in anything. I had been disappointed so many times. Could this be any different? *Dateline* had given me a brief high, but I remained depressed somewhere between the mountain of pain and the pit of despair. Could I stand up again? With April's help, perhaps I could. There was hope. We could change the world.

10. Unlocking the Past for the Future

I spent the day after the *Dateline* show thinking about losing everything I had held dear; I was seriously troubled. I was feeling abandoned all over again: my new family had deserted me just like I thought the old one had. Even though I had been vindicated on national television, I still felt alone, with guilt hanging over me. I needed a serious outlet to help me work through all that anguish and regret. I needed something to help make me want to stand up and fight once again. I needed a purpose.

April had told me that writing things down helped her to clarify them and that starting a journal might help me. She had given me one, but I hadn't cracked it open. I had been toying with the idea of writing a book about my experiences, but it didn't seem like a bright one. Who'd ever want to read it? Plus, I don't write well. It's always been a struggle because of all the interruptions in my schooling, a lack of interest in reading, and my ADHD. But a journal was not nearly as daunting as all that. Anything was better than nothing. So I began to write.

While digging into my memory and psyche, writing about all the torturous times in my life, I came to a crossroads. Should I go ahead and attempt a book, or just keep my miseries buried? If I did write one, would it ever get published? How do you find a publisher? I wondered, too, if my family would even care. I had been standoffish with my family, because I felt I never seemed to be good enough for their love and support. I had given them enough trouble. It was childish, I know, but I never grew up in this area. When I was eighteen years old, a therapist at McLean Hospital told me that in some areas I was like a thirty-year-old woman, but in others, I was stuck back in time as a little, twelve-year-old girl. I felt insulted at the time, but over the years, I had come to understand what she said to me that day. Yes, I'm a living, breathing psychological time warp.

My personal social skills had never caught up to me as an adult. In business, it was a different story. My motto for myself there was "fake it until you make it." People could only judge me by what I did with my company. No one knew of my demons from the past. I hadn't even acknowledged them to myself until I started writing about them fourteen years later.

In business I had felt powerful, and so I was. I had a staff of thirty-two living souls whose livelihoods depended on me. I had revenue of over a million dollars. I'd owned property worth millions of dollars more. I was the chief cook, and bottle washer, and I wore the hat of CEO well. It made me powerful.

On a personal level, though, I was a weakling. I was dying to be perfect. I would make excuses not to see my family by saying to myself I wasn't skinny enough, I wasn't educated enough, I wasn't successful enough for their love and attention. The real reason was that I didn't want to be hurt again. Hey, if my mother could let me down and choose a guy over me, then what was I worth? I wasn't important enough. I didn't want to let anyone in my family ever hurt me again by abandoning me. I know this isn't fair to my family. I only wish my father's family had found me all those years ago, before my stepfather inflicted so much pain and suffering. For a long time, I hadn't even known that they had ever tried. I only found out when I was into my early thirties, still drowning myself in self-pity and spewing it all out into written words. I had started to write it all down. I wrote for days that grew into weeks, and through that exercise I began to want to know my whole past, especially the parts hidden by my psyche. By then, I knew how badly I wanted to let people know what had happened: my story.

Once April became aware that I thought that the journal could be the basis for a published book, she offered to have a go at writing the thing for me. People would look at us slightly confused and maybe amused when we related what we were up to. They would say, "I didn't know April was a writer." She'd laughingly retort that no one is until they just do it. I had already taken my typed journal pages to a counselor at Florida Atlantic University when I was laboriously finishing my bachelor's degree. She thought the story was engaging and said she couldn't wait to see the rest. She said my vocabulary—that is, my cussing—might bother people, but it also got the point across, and at times it was hysterical; it was humor hidden amid all the angst. With that wholehearted vote of approval, I decided I wanted to move forward.

Once my desire to write a book had solidified, April became tenacious. She became the driving force behind this book. She was merciless about making me find out what had happened in the times I didn't remember well. She frequently reminds me of my old friend Marilyn, all bossy and everything, but it's for all the right reasons.

We began to write together. I shared my memories, bad and good, at a level I had never experienced in my life before. I'd been in therapy of some sort for almost a third of my thirty-two years. Nothing a therapist has done compares to April reaching into the very recesses of my mind and tearing down walls with patient, constant prodding. She was tenacious, yet kind and extremely thorough. We were not on a therapist's clock; we were on a mission. She tore my memory wide open, and I will not kid you, it was terrifying and extremely painful—for both of us. It was also enlightening. I had been missing a huge chunk of my life!

One night, we'd taken a break from writing and had gone out partying with friends until the wee hours. We reached home as the sun was rising. April had given me a place to stay, since my entire financial world had collapsed and my home was in foreclosure. I was extremely depressed, and all the alcohol hadn't helped. I began lamenting my woes and bawling about loneliness and having no family. Again!

April flipped out on me. She said that this was quite enough and that I needed to grow up. She looked me straight in my weepy, bloodshot eyes and told me I must give my family more credit. They hadn't cut me off! It was the reverse: I had cut them off first. What an epiphany! It wasn't them, it was me.

That very day, scared and unsure, I began cautiously reaching out through Facebook to those family members I could find. I wasn't brave enough to just pick up the telephone. On Facebook, I could still hide in case there were no responses. I'd seen my relatives periodically at family reunions, but I had been completely reserved. Nobody ever brought up my past. I'll give them enough credit to say they were waiting for a signal from me that it was OK to speak. I had arrived at a point where I was waving the white flag. The past was killing me, and I couldn't take it anymore. It was time to speak up and ask questions, because I needed to find out what had happened.

One thing was really tormenting April. She has a very protective personality, and it was driving her crazy not knowing why Butch had never paid for his crimes. We'd taken him to court, but what was the deal? How in the hell had he gotten away with it for those two whole years before he'd died unexpectedly? She thought two years was a long time to wait and that death was way too easy on him. She wished he were alive just so she could throttle him herself. I didn't know why there was no legal reprisal against Butch. I just remember going to his funeral, seeing him in his casket, and rejoicing that he could never hurt anyone anymore. That day is indelibly imprinted on my memory, because it was the last time I spoke to my stepsisters. They asked me if I was happy now that I'd killed their dad. What a vicious thing to say at a funeral.

I remember standing there, taking in what they had said, and the feeling of rejection was horrible. April wanted to know exactly when this had happened, but I couldn't tell her, because I just couldn't recall. I remembered feeling overwhelmed by grief, thinking that it must have somehow been my fault, and guilty, because without my help, my mother would have to shoulder everything on her own. I no longer felt welcome to help her. That's about the clearest memory I have of that two-year period when I must have been between fifteen and eighteen years old.

My cousin Jamie was the first to respond to my Facebook request, and he shone a huge spotlight into the black hole of my past. He's the one who always had my back when his sister Taneasha was after me when we were little kids. He had kept in touch by phone from time to time, more than anyone else in my family, but just with simple courtesies.

When Jamie called me, we connected more fully, because I gave him the sign that I was ready to talk about the past. I'm glad he was first, because I had always felt safe with him.

He called while I was standing on April's tiny front porch, looking at the swaying trees across the street in the park. She was grumpy, taking a break from writing, wanting to get her hands around my stepfather's neck, and was sitting and smoking a cigar. It was a muggy day, even for Florida in springtime, and it was threatening to rain. The gloomy weather, dense with black clouds, was adding pressure to my already heavy mood. I felt that all my past had ganged up on me and that I was sinking in a morass of lost memories, sort of like being in a grave and buried up to the nose, suffocating under a mound of dark thoughts.

Jamie and I had been talking for only a minute or so when April rudely interrupted my conversation to tell me to ask about Butch not going to jail. She was tired of waiting to hear whatever excuse the state of Massachusetts had used to let him remain free his last couple of years. I asked Jamie. There was a pregnant pause, and then he let the bomb drop. He told me that Butch had been indicted; he'd been facing trial, and he was going to pay. He just died first — within two weeks of the indictment.

April's cigar dropped out of her mouth, burning her slacks as her jaw flopped open, and of course, I was speechless. We both asked Jamie to repeat what he had said while staring at each other in amazement. All these years, I'd thought Butch had hung around worry free after I left. I thought he'd simply passed away for some reason or other, two years after I got the temporary restraining order. I was sure wrong. April was ecstatic, and the state was off the hook. Butch hadn't gotten away with it after all, and while he didn't go to jail, he'd gone somewhere where God could set the punishment and make him pay.

We spoke for quite a while. Thankfully, we had Jamie on speakerphone so April could hear. Hearing that Butch had died just days after being indicted left me dazed and confused, and then I was sobbing, releasing so many years of pent-up emotion. I had always thought that no one had believed me, because Mom had made me lie and say that Butch had never tried anything or done anything to me. How could it be that did I not know that he was going to be tried in court? What a mess my memories were. Jamie was shocked that I didn't know and said I should speak to his mom. He had been really young at the time. Reconnection with the family was underway, and I was ripping the old, musty, hidden bones out of the closet.

When I got off of the phone, April and I were dancing around like two kids celebrating the last day of school. Looking into the park, we saw that God had chosen to blow all the dark clouds away. The sky was now blue, and there was a fresh breeze blowing through the trees just like the balmy, gentle currents driving darkness from my mind and drying the tears on my cheeks.

Jamie's mom, Auntie Estelle, spoke to me later and confirmed that my stepfather had been indicted by the state of Massachusetts for his crimes, but she said he actually died within a week of the indictment, very unexpectedly. I was floored again by that hit. How had I lived all these years, thinking he'd been there with my mother and siblings for two years longer than he was? There was a big gap in my memory. What else had happened that I didn't remember? It is just so strange knowing a considerable period of your life is AWOL. What is worse, though, is that I might never have known had April and I not been writing this book.

Jamie and Aunt Estelle were the first of many calls. In the following days, I reconstructed a vast supply of memories based upon conversations I held with those relatives who had been there for me all those years ago. I felt an illuminating and healing sensation from reconnecting with them and from finally understanding that they didn't all hate me for what I'd done to them back then.

One of the people I spoke with was my crazy cousin Taneasha. She literally had been my knight in shining armor, swooping in and stealing me from school and hiding me from my parents and hers. We talked about the day she showed up at my school after my parents had come and taken me away from her mom's house. She told me how determined she had been to get me out of there. She had worked up the nerve and swaggered into the school office like she belonged there and knew exactly what she was doing. It was quite a feat for someone only nineteen years old. She would've had even more cheeky authority at that age than she'd shown at eleven. I imagine that she marched into that office, slapped a hand on a cocked hip, jutted out those lips, drilled the secretary to the chair with her amazing, daring eyes, and demanded I be brought to the office. "Family business," she'd say. I can just picture it!

We were laughing on the phone about our audacity, but what Taneasha couldn't see were the hot tears of gratefulness rolling down my cheeks as I wept quietly at the memory of my rescue. My rescue that day meant the difference between life and death for me. I don't think Taneasha will ever be able to grasp the significance of my escape from school that day, or how much it had affected my life. She is my hero. I will never forget it.

Another person who I friended on Facebook was my cousin Gary Ewing. I don't recall being around him since I was about seven years old. He had a great smile, a hearty laugh, and I remember him quite well. He took me out one time, way back when while I was visiting my grandmother, and he bought me a musical instrument. At the time I was ecstatic, just because he was paying attention to me. I think my grandmother was mortified by his gift. She was a classical music teacher and ran a nonprofit organization for music enrichment. She knew this instrument was a toy but didn't say a word to me. Yet I could see it in her eyes that she thought it was silly. You have to understand. She is a great woman, a wonderful grandmother, but none of us would take piano or violin lessons from her, because she was way too tough. We were scared to death of her. Gary was just so excited that I was happy that I don't know if he noticed my grandmother's look. I'm glad if he didn't. It was a gift given from the heart and received with the joy it was intended to bring.

Gary is a comedian, and I thought he might know someone we could send the book to for publishing. I was embarrassed to ask, but April insisted I talk to him. She laughed outright when I showed her his picture. She is quite sure she had seen him perform in person at some point during her old traveling days. Wouldn't it be something if it was around the same time I remember seeing him last? One night after putting my younger siblings to sleep, I saw him on television performing live. When Gary came on, I told my stepsisters to come see, telling them that he was my cousin. I think they thought I was crazy. Who was I to know someone on TV? I couldn't forget him, because he'd brought such simple joy into my life once.

I really didn't want to impose, but April was insistent. We needed to find someone to print our book, didn't we? She had been such a huge support to me. How could I say no to her? She had picked me up off the ground when I didn't think life was worth living. She spoke encouraging words to me when I couldn't hear. April held me at my weakest moments when I couldn't stand alone, when I thought no one in the world cared. She'd been right so far with her advice, so I decided to listen again.

I called Gary that night. I was so afraid. What if he didn't remember me or want to talk to me? What if he didn't care about what I had to say?

Gary answered the phone, and his voice sounded so familiar. He has this sweet voice that no one could forget. It instantly brought me back to comfortable memories of him, as if I were seven years old again. We talked about everything that had happened, from my being abused, to Haile, and to *Dateline*. I didn't go into details of the abuse. I had never told any of my father's family exactly what had happened. All they knew was that I was sexually abused. I then began to tell him I was writing a book and asked if he could help me. He said he would contact a couple of his friends who had written books to see if they could help.

He then began to tell me about his cause, Stop the War on Fathers, and the need for fathers to be involved in their children's lives, even if they aren't perfect. He asked me if I thought my father had been in my life enough. He said that if he and his family had been more involved in my life, the abuse might not have happened to me at all, or it could've ended sooner. He explained about all the other children who are abused because they don't have their natural fathers to protect them. It was a heady subject.

I told him I *didn't* think my dad had been allowed around me enough because Butch wouldn't allow it. My stepfather had us isolated from both sides of the family. Gary was right; I thought that if I had been closer to my loving family, my real dad, I would have had someone to talk to. I might have had someone to defend me. He wished me luck, asked me sincerely to keep in touch, and we ended the call.

A few weeks later, I called again. He said his friends hadn't gotten back to him yet but to send him what I had so far. April didn't want anyone closely involved to see what had been written before it was done. That invites way too many opinions. I was nervous, because I didn't want any of my family to read the book before I had it published. You must be asking why. Well, first, I didn't want my mother to start working on me, telling me a book was a very bad idea and that I should burn it, and second, I didn't want anyone in my family to tell me to delete *this* part over here, or if not *this*, then *that* should go, and who needs to know *this* anyway, Kathryn?

I felt the book could speak to different people on different levels. I didn't want anyone, let alone family, to tell me how I should have felt or that I was exposing myself — and them — too much. I feel that the reader should have my whole truth. This was essential. This was huge for me.

We decided to trust Gary and e-mailed the first few chapters. He responded back very quickly.

The following are excerpts from his e-mail reply:

THIS IS A TOUGH READ! It is so sad that this happened to you. I remember in 1992 I told your aunts and your father to try to see if they could contact you but they said they didn't know where you were! I told them since Larry was your father he could track you down by your school records. But sometimes a father needs a court order to obtain this information. The sad part of this is that we were all looking for you! It's sad to say but once a mother makes up her mind that the father's family will never have any contact with the children, there is very little a father can do!!!!! Even Uncle Mannie and Aunt Helen were looking for you! FAMILY COURT IS NO HELP…. In fact in my opinion family court is partly responsible. They are the biggest culprits in this entire mess. Go look at the court records and see for yourself. The judge most likely did nothing but enforce "child support." He/she couldn't have cared less if your father and his family had a relationship with you! […]

And you should put a chapter in about family court! Moreover, all studies have shown that sexual abuse of a child (by a step parent) almost never happens when the biological father is either in the household or is involved in the child's life. This would have never happened to you if "family court" granted your father joint custody and enforced a parenting time (visitation) order. I've got to stop now because I getting angry!!!!!!!!!!!!!!!!!

I read the e-mail and was shocked. He'd asked my family in 1992 to find me, maybe even before the abuse had started. Someone had actually cared enough to look for me. Then I asked myself: had they found me, then what if? What if the courts had told my mother that my father's side of the family had a right to see me? Would I have been saved from all the pain and suffering I went through? I wish they had found me. I wish the system had let them, or that they had tried harder. I feel the system let me down in that way as a child.

The weirdest thing about finally speaking with my family is that every one of them remembers like it was yesterday. It's as if they all had their memories tucked away in a secret vault, just waiting for me to turn the key and release them.

As I began filling in the void of those two years, I felt like I was healing on some levels. I felt vindicated by some of the things I learned and buried by others. I was happy with the responses I'd gotten, but felt that they were too little, too late. Never mind that I had waited so long to ask. My emotions were a giant teeter-totter, and I really didn't want to be on it. One minute I'd be high and the next low. I'd be happy and miserable, all at the same time. I'd been seeing a therapist since Haile's death as well as a psychiatrist. They were treating me in critical mode for the loss of Haile, but nobody, me included, was discussing the abuse. When April got wind of that, I got a huge talking-to. She wanted to know what the hell I had been doing the last year and a half, wasting time and money on people who couldn't connect the dots. She was furious that they didn't tie together my huge, depressive funk over the loss of Haile to the loss of my own childhood.

She ranted at me for hours about not taking responsibility for my own healing. She badgered me to tears about finding a competent doctor, because she wasn't equipped to help me alone. April had helped me tremendously, but I needed professional help to provide me with the tools necessary to work through my issues.

I needed to address all my issues, get back on steady ground, and (how many times have I said it) finally begin to heal the child in me who'd been tortured, abused, and abandoned. It wasn't going to be easy or quick, but as April would say, "It damn well needs to be thorough."

A doctor could give me the tools; however, only I could carry me back up my mountain of pain. It was time again for me to stand on my own two feet and to toil.

11. Striving for Triumph

I forced myself to struggle up from my psychologically prone position. I grabbed at the ideas of the book and the alarm system to use them as crutches for my stumbling start at a new life. April said we could do both. I chose to believe her.

We had only known each other for two weeks. I felt like she had been around forever. In that short time, she had broken down many of the barriers I had built around me as far back as childhood. She made me receptive to true friendship, with no strings attached. She had shared her best friends with me, encouraging them to accept me for who I was and not what I had been. She opened my eyes about my family loving me and not expecting me to be anything but happy. She was amazing, and now she had given me something very concrete to live and strive for. I would tell my story in the hope it might touch someone else. I would help her, with my knowledge of pre-schools, to design an alarm system that would work to save children's lives. Maybe I actually could triumph over the tragedies in my life that had stolen my innocence.

Incredibly, the book already had a title, chapter outlines, and a theme. April wasn't messing around. She spent days on the initial prologue and first chapter, trying to set the stage for my life's story. I was blown away by her retention of my verbal and typed feelings. It was as though she had climbed right inside my skin and was experiencing me.

She had also contacted her father, Jerry Braun, about the alarm. He is an old military guy with plenty of brains and experience with mechanical processes. She wanted to see if he could help her design a prototype so she could file for a patent. He was reticent at first. He explained about his health not being what it should be and that he was seventy-five years old—too old to be considering such an undertaking. She got off the phone with him and grinned. I was sad that he didn't seem to want to help. What was she grinning about?

"Well, that'll get that old Braun brain percolating. My mom is going to owe me big-time for giving him something to do besides sitting around and listening to all the political assholes on the news telling him how bad his life is," April said. "And he can run rings around any forty-year-old person I know. He just thinks he should still have the energy of a twenty-year-old!"

"But he said he couldn't help," I reminded her. I was a bit confused by her glee; she was literally rubbing her hands together in anticipation, with an avaricious grin on her face and her nose all scrunched up. She looked like a scrooge who'd just won the lottery.

"He won't be able to help himself. He is smart as hell, and the chance to help little kids will override anything else. He loves kids!" she said and went back to writing.

"I hope so…but I am not too optimistic."

"No, you are a natural-born pessimist. Just trust me on this one, Miss Negative Nancy. We do not want to have to lay out ten thousand dollars on a mechanical drawing for a patent concept. He'll do it. It just has to seem like his idea. Stop worrying," she said. "And besides, if he gets too bogged down, my niece Sarah can help. She is a brilliant mechanical engineering student at Wright State University. She works full time in the plasma technology experimentation and research lab over on Wright-Patterson Air Force Base. I got us covered. Can you turn the meat over for me? We have to come up with good corporate names for all this junk." She buried her nose in her laptop again, and I had to laugh. Talk about multitasking! She was writing my memoir, chatting about patents, mumbling to herself about corporate names, and cooking her hand-pressed breakfast meat all at once.

The days marched forward as my time at FAU drew to a close. I had a much more positive outlook lately, yet the demons were never far below the surface, with April dredging everything up for the book. Lorinda and Barbara were both a huge help in getting me through the last days of the school-year curriculum. April helped in more practical ways, making sure I ate and slept well, and she was still chauffeuring me around. I would find her after class in the smoking section outside the main food court, puffing away.

She'd be at a picnic table lit by dappled sunlight typing busily, her face screwed up into a unique mask she wore whenever she was thinking. I'd stand and watch her for a bit before interrupting, wondering why God had been kind enough to send her my way. If I had not gotten drunk that night and she hadn't been nice enough to worry about a stranger getting home, we might never have met. I probably wouldn't have survived the last week before *Dateline* without her. She'd give me a big, wolfish grin whenever she saw me and would ask me to read the latest excerpts from the book.

At times, I didn't want to. Her interpretations of my experiences were eerie and discombobulating. She wrote so much of what I felt. She would talk to me a lot, but it was her retention of my answers that blew my mind. She remembered everything I told her. Some things were impossible for me to read more than once. I couldn't stand the parts about my stepfather abusing me. I'd die a little every time I read about my mom choosing him. If I felt that strongly, I sincerely hoped others would too, and maybe by unveiling my spirit, others would learn that they can stand up to oppressors. The humorous sections I could read again and again, chuckling in places and sometimes laughing out loud. I loved every word, painful or not.

After the first few chapters were well drafted and written up, April suggested we get an opinion and contact Dr. Oliver at FAU.

April wanted Dr. Oliver's input on the direction of the story, since she had published a memoir and several other books. I had mentioned the book to her before, and I agreed to e-mail her. Dr. Oliver offered to look over what we had so far and to give us an honest opinion. We set up an appointment with her at her office on the FAU campus down in Davie, just west of Fort Lauderdale.

I was a nervous wreck as we drove down with the printed manuscript and my journal pages. April insisted I give her both. All I could think of was that virulent shade of red all over my school papers, infecting my written innermost thoughts. I knew my version was atrocious. I was just vomiting words onto the page as fast as possible without regard for spelling, grammar, or punctuation. Dr. Oliver would have a field day with her red pen, and it made me shudder.

"Are you too cold?" April asked.

"No, I just know how bad she is going to tear up my writing," I said. She looked at me and quit adjusting the air-conditioning vents.

"That really is not our first concern here. We will explain what your pages represent. If nothing else, she will feel the sheer emotion in your text. The structure doesn't matter right now," she said.

"You don't know her," I said.

"Just relax. She knows this is not ready for publication. Besides, if you're nervous, imagine my worries," she said as she accelerated into the HOV lane. "I haven't had someone proof anything I've written since you were about three years old. I'm the one who should be freaking out. My spelling, grammar, and punctuation are horrendous, and I know it—and pretty soon, so will she." She laughed after that and changed the subject to the alarm system names we had been tossing around.

We would sit with a notepad and blurt out any words that came to mind that seemed fitting. Some definitely were not, and we'd both crack up, mostly at my attempts. April called it brainstorming. I enjoyed making my brain work. We had about fifteen good ideas when she started shortening everything to acronyms. April was adamant that she wanted the name short but to mean a mouthful. We argued about it all the way on the fifty-minute drive. She laughed when we arrived on campus.

"What are you laughing at?" I asked.

"Nothing like a good verbal tussle to ward off the nerves," she said. I laughed too. She was always taking care of me.

Dr. Oliver showed up that day in tan linen slacks and a blouse, sporting a no-nonsense hat that matched her pants. She has such a huge personality that I nearly choked on stifled laughter at the sight of April towering over her in her office when they met; they were quite a mismatch, considering the obvious difference in size and personas. I felt about five years old in the professor's presence. April looked like an adult and acted like a professional. None of her nerves were showing.

Dr. Oliver's warm welcome was sincere, and she said she would be glad to help me. I handed over the two documents with shaking, sweaty hands while explaining the shortcomings of my version. She ignored that comment as she breezed through April's outline, prologue, and first chapters.

"You have a nice start here," she said. "The chapter outlines are thorough and the prologue is interesting — though incomplete, I assume. I think what you need to do is get the whole story on paper and then rework the prologue. You have to capture the reader immediately. Provide a synopsis of what will happen. Tie it together with the main points of the story and emphasize being on *Dateline*. Most people will never be on the news in their lifetimes, and it will tantalize them." She rifled through my journal notes while I held my breath.

"One of our concerns is the levity in different parts of the story," April said. She leaned forward with her arms on her knees, hands dangling, wide open to suggestions.

Dr. Oliver replied, "I believe that the human condition is a broad spectrum of emotions, and we would not survive strife if we couldn't come out the other side laughing. Nobody will want to read a story that is only depressing. The levity is a strong tool to break up any monotony. It is necessary to tell any good story by encompassing all human emotions, so keep that in mind as you write." She explained in more depth the need to make the prologue more like a thesis statement. She said she would evaluate the story again for me once it was finished, and in the meantime, she would review in depth what we had given her already. We were to come back in a few weeks to pick up further suggestions.

Then she leaned back in her chair and asked how I was doing. I explained all the recent changes in my life. I talked about my excitement for inventing an alarm and the emotional upheaval engendered by the book. She nodded her head in understanding, and April stood up, politely concluding the meeting. We said our good-byes and thanks, shook the professor's hand, and left.

I sighed heavily as we boarded the elevator. April looked at me questioningly.

"Man, am ever I glad that is over. Phew!" I said while inspecting the wet stains in my armpits and under my breasts. I had been in a flop sweat the entire time we were in there.

"You act like she is some hideous gargoyle primed to pounce on you," she said. "I thought she was very nice and not at all intimidating." She chuckled at my antics as I attempted to locate all my sweaty spots, including the crack of my butt. I was such a mess.

"That's because you aren't dependent on a grade. And she obviously liked your work!" I cried.

"Kathryn, you aren't dependent on her for a grade either—not anymore," she calmly pointed out. She was right. I still high-tailed it to the car liked a startled deer. She laughed at me the whole way. I really can be childish, as she also pointed out.

We sat quietly as the air conditioner struggled to combat the trapped heat in the van. It made me think of Haile left for hours in a kind of oven, and I disappeared into the past. I came back some time later when April figured I'd had enough. She shook my arm and asked what the matter was.

"I was thinking of Haile," I said.

"Was it because of the hot van?" she asked.

"Yes! April, it amazes me how you figure me out so easily. Thank you for caring enough to pay attention. I don't know what I would've done without you recently," I said.

"You're welcome," she said. We drove on in a comfortable silence, both of us fully present.

We tracked down Teri Catlin that night at one of her concerts. It was a sort of celebration for making the book official — not that we needed an excuse to go see her. We had done so a dozen times the last few weeks. Her music made us both feel so much better. She was at the Bamboo Room in Lake Worth. She sang, and we drank. I videotaped her songs on my phone. When she played "American Girl," I knew it was meant for me. When her guitar solo arrived, she jumped down from the stage and approached me. She sidled right up in my face and rocked out her rendition of "Let It Be," by the Beatles. In the weeks to follow, I watched that video countless times as the music bore into my soul and her face lit up my heart. Teri is someone else I have to be very thankful for.

She met us at The Bar Lake Worth after her gig. She brought several friends with her who were visiting from California. We partied there until closing time. Missi the bartender and April's two friends, Eric and Tasha, along with Teri's crew, decided to move the party to April's house. Penny wanted to go, but she still had to close up, and she wanted a relatively early night. (Considering it was after two thirty already, that was a bit of a joke.)

We all descended on April's tiny Lantana house and over-flowed onto the porch. I badgered Teri into letting me listen to her new songs on the CD player in April's van. She obliged me. I had it cranked up so loud that April had to keep coming out to tell me to turn it down so I didn't disturb the neighbors. I was obstinate and didn't attend to her. Everyone out there with me was enjoying the music too and egged me on to keep the music going. I didn't care what anyone thought tonight and was feeling no pain. I'd turn it right back up as soon as April walked away. She was pretty loaded that night and was ready to commit hara-kiri — but on me, not herself. She came out with eyes blazing for the last time at a quarter to six as the stereo went silent. I had completely run down the van's battery. I laughed sheepishly as the guys all rushed to help jump-start her van. When the van was running again and I wanted to listen some more, the CD was gone. I figured April had swiped it to enforce some quiet.

By the time I went to sleep, the sun was up, and we had three extra people in the house sleeping on the futon and air mattresses. This was such a new experience for me. I had always been in such sheltered relationships. I had never had a horde of friends who just liked to hang out. Here was a group of people who wanted to have fun and knew how to go about it. I loved it.

April and I sat in stupefied silence most of the day, just recovering. She grinned at me and told me she was way too old for all these shenanigans. Everyone had left, and she needed to get back to work. I just wanted to sit and enjoy the memory of Teri singing to me. I needed to relive the entire acceptance April's friends had shown me. I didn't want to dredge up the past, but I had to.

The book was taking shape. April's dad called and said he had some ideas for the alarm. She gave me a knowing grin and I laughed. She had been right. He wanted to help. Now it was his idea.

The next weeks were a hodgepodge of memories and awakenings. Our alarm was becoming a reality. We would truly be able to help children, and my heart swelled in my breast. I could really become an advocate for children.

At the end of April, we packed up the van and headed north to Ohio. The technical drawing for the alarm was near completion, and April wanted to sit down in person with her father and niece to discuss the final concepts for the patent. Also, her other niece, Rachel, was getting married, and she wanted to be there for that.

I cannot stand long trips in a car, but April tried her best to make me comfortable. She laid all of the van's stow-and-go seats down and took a twin air mattress and wedged it in the back. She had a nifty little travel DVD player and a cooler full of junk food. I'd have to be crazy not to know I was like a queen traveling in state. Nevertheless, after twelve hours, I was a nutcase. I am ADHD, and trees and billboards couldn't cut through my misery from inactivity. It felt something like I was crawling out of my skin into a monochromatic world void of all stimulation.

Couldn't we hurry things up? April had started to feel my pain by the time I'd asked if we were there yet for the thousandth time.

I finally just passed out from nervous exhaustion. April calmly drove on. We made the eleven-hundred-and-thirty-mile drive in record time; the record was that I hadn't totally lost my mind.

As soon as we got there and the hugging and kissing was over, April's mom said she wanted her to find two four-leaf clovers for her nephew's impending twins, because she has a magic eye. He and his wife had recently lost a baby to a very rare disease, so the family was ecstatic about the new pregnancy. So I went straight from a mind-numbing voyage to scrabbling around in the weeds for clover, and I was fit to be tied. As much as I love kids, I was up in arms. The idea of driving for twenty-six hours, then being forced to do something as interesting as watching cement dry, made me feel a bit murderous. When April decides to do something, though, she applies her whole being to the task. After two hours of staring at clover patches, she very well could have been my first murder victim.

By the time April convened a meeting of the minds, I was ripe for mischief. Her dad, Sarah, and I all huddled at the dinner table. They could've told me the sky was blue, and I would have argued that it was purple. I was very interested in the alarm, but I could not make myself focus after the last two days. I made them work their wearied brains off to make me happy. I regretted it later, but at the moment, I felt justified. I registered every inane complaint I had about the existing alarms. They took my worries to heart and worked out ways to combat the problems.

At one point, April's mom was giggling in the kitchen, and I had to know why. April finally got up to go see why her mom was so tickled. She had a very familiar look on her face: the very recognizable mask that April often wore. She was thinking something and was clearly amused at it.

"What's the deal, Mom?" April asked.

"Look at your dad!" she said.

"I am...and what is your point?"

"Really, look at him. He has never before been bossed around by three women, and it's cracking me up!"

April turned around and laughed out loud. The humor of the situation grabbed hold of her, and then the meeting was thankfully over. She could no longer concentrate on the problem at hand.

My generation is a media-dependent one, and I finally did get an electronic fix from April's parents' television. It dawned on me that I had been living for weeks without an idiot box. I had seriously missed it and channel surfing. How can you live without a TV? I don't know how, but April sure did. She grew up in a time when you created your own fun from something called an imagination.

We had a very good visit with April's family. They are a down-to-earth Midwestern clan that enjoys a good laugh as much as a good meal. I'll bet I put on ten pounds from the plethora of carbs presented to us. We met with her dad a few more times before we drove back south. I really felt we were onto a great concept for the alarm. April had been right; her father and Sarah were both brilliant. I felt a little intimidated with the three of them, but knew I definitely had a say in the process. I was excited to see the finished product.

Heading back to the sunshine state, April broke up the drive for me, thank God. We stopped for the night in Atlanta, checking into the Westin Peachtree Plaza. It is one of her favorite hotels, and she's been in quite a few. The next day, she surprised me by taking me to the Martin Luther King Jr. National Historical Site. She had told me she did not see people categorized by color, and now I really believed her. She has an enormous respect for MLK Jr. She could recite most of his massive contributions to this country. She said she wished she could have been a part of the Freedom Riders. She would have taken her knocks with pride. I saw her now on a very different level. It is one thing to say you are not prejudiced, and quite another actually not being it. My heart swelled with pride for my new friend. April is amazing.

When we got home, my thoughts about the success of our alarm plans helped me to deal with the frustrations of school. I wanted a degree, and I was about to get one. I just had to take about thirty more tests, and I'd be done. Lorinda helped center my efforts. Barbara helped with research. And April was just herself. She unconsciously had taken the reins of my life and was steering me up a path to success, with my permission. They were all wonderful.

On May 4, 2012, April drove me to the FAU campus. We were both awash in smiles. I was about to walk across the stage to receive my diploma. I had missed that important experience when I dropped out of high school. I was elated. It had taken fourteen years to get to this day, against all odds. It was huge! We sat in the car with happy tears shimmering on our eyelids. She kissed me gently and said how proud she was to share this day with me.

I stood in the hot Florida sun and adjusted my cap. Such a little thing meant so much. I could now look my family square in their eyes and feel accomplished.

As the ceremony progressed, I was filled with pride. I had survived so much. I was standing strongly on two feet and growing by leaps and bounds. I had amazing friends to share the moment with. I was truly happy. I was finally and unconditionally proud of myself.

When I mounted the stairs to the stage, Teri screamed her encouragement, and I paused to enjoy the moment. The stage was mine, and I worked it. When I was handed the diploma folder, my heart was overjoyed. I had done it. I had become officially educated.

I had a permanent grin tattooed on my face. Life was so good at this moment. We headed out into the sunshine and took some pictures to commemorate my evolution.

Those photos were ultimately used to create the background picture for the American Girl Experiences website. Lorinda, Teri, April, and I created a diverse collage of American women. We were all survivors, and we rejoiced in our growth. We understood what it takes to make it as a modern American woman.

After the high of the graduation ceremony, I was struck by a moribund sense of guilt. I had made it, but Haile would never get the chance to succeed. I would do whatever it took to make sure that a loss like hers would never happen again. And right then and there, I promised myself never to let her death overpower my happiness again. I had to understand that grief is healthy, but only up to a point.

April and I hired a website designer and began the process of formalizing our corporate ideals. We spent days wrestling with names and the verbiage describing our efforts. On May 7, 2012, we filed for incorporation with the state of Florida. We were now officially known as American Girl Experiences, LLC. The acronym is AGE—and it fit because we were both coming of age. We had spread our wings and were preparing to take flight.

Over the next week, we finalized the names for the DBA corporations needed for the alarm, video, and other safety products. It was very exciting. Once again, I had gone from being a homeless waif to a business owner.

On June 12, we filed for our patent. All the aggravation of finalizing the engineering drawing was done. We had a very viable product. Royal Craig, an attorney at Ober/Kaler in Baltimore, was handling the patent application for us. He said the drawing was 100 percent correct. April's dad was so proud.

On June 18, April and I began filming a video to put on Indiegogo.com, which our website designer had introduced us to. It is a fundraising site for independent companies and individuals who need money. We were mesmerized by the stories we saw on the site. We thought there could be a huge opportunity to raise our manufacturing capital with the site's help.

April had been busy writing the book, so she left the video script up to me—at least as much as someone can who is as anal-retentive as she is. She'd be immersed in the book when she'd pipe up with significant changes to my efforts. She was brutal with me about my enthusiasm in reading the video's text. I had to read that script about five thousand times, and she still wasn't happy. I knew where she was coming from, but her aggravation just shut me down. She has much more faith in me than I do, but it didn't help. She wanted it passionate and perfect, and I wasn't prepared to perform either way.

When we finally dragged out the video camera on its tripod, I was a nervous wreck. We planned the setting to incorporate the park across the street from her house. This was about saving kids, and the park made sense.

We got up at the crack of dawn to avoid the heat. April fussed around with camera angles for about twenty minutes before she was satisfied. I was melting. The many takes for the filming lasted forever. I read my part, and April fussed.

We marched back to her house and uploaded the raw video. It completely sucked. Neither of us had noticed the breeze whistling around our scene. You couldn't hear what I was saying for the rustle of the wind. She looked at me and just burst out laughing.

"Even the gods knew that sucked and are determined to make us redo it," she said. She wiped the streaming tears of mirth from her eyes as I wiped the tears of regret from mine. I didn't know if I could do any better, and her badgering me and making fun didn't help. I never felt I read well, and now it was evident.

"Aw, come on!" she said, "take it for what it's worth. You are not an actress, and I am not an award-winning director. Just believe in what we are trying to do, and you'll be fine." Her gentle smile relaxed me.

As we prepared to retake the video, she remembered a beach umbrella she had that might stifle the sound of the wind. She lugged it out of the storage room, and we dragged everything back across the street.

We were well on our way to completion when some guy got on a swing, and it squeaked so loud that April about shit herself. She hopped out from under the umbrella like some manic troll guarding a bridge and asked the guy to please be quiet. He sheepishly walked away.

The murderous look on her face when she turned back to me was too much for my sense of humor. I started snickering and couldn't stop. The humor was infectious, and she barked out a laugh. We were both taking this way too seriously. She tracked the guy down and apologized. She explained what we were doing, and he asked if he could watch.

So I started over yet again. I read better, but April was still frustrated by my lack of enthusiasm. My description of the alarm was boring, and we both knew it. We carried everything back to the house so she could clean up and redo the technical description.

By the time we returned to the park to continue, it was just plain hot outside. I laughed at the vision of April's pants stuck in her butt crack and the sheen of sweat sparkling on her face. I wasn't the only one who was miserable now. She restarted about twenty times before we managed a good take. I could see the sweat pooled on her lined face. I knew she was as wretched as me. We sat in the shade of the umbrella and talked about redoing my stuff. She'd grin at our suffering, and I'd just laugh.

I stood up by the slide this time and was determined to just do it full out and give my all. It was much better than before, but still very mechanical. I was at the very end of the three-minute speech when a car stopped on the road and honked its horn repeatedly.

"Are you kidding me? Right now?" April bellowed. "What in the world does she need?" The lady asked for directions, and we told her where she should go. I wandered into the cover of some shade. April was sweating in places she didn't even know she had. I was laughing at her, and she knew it.

"Oh, my God. Everyone is conspiring against us!" she said. "Let us just get this piece done, and I will leave you alone forever." She huddled back under the umbrella and pointed at me to go. The speech flowed. I was still automaton-like, but it sounded better. I was just speaking the part about our never wanting anyone to see a newscast about dead kids on a bus when an ice-cream truck meandered through the neighborhood. The music from the truck changed the atmosphere, but April waved me on to continue. She did not want to make me redo all of this again. I didn't want to either. "That really sucked, but you were fine. You could not ask for more contradictory sounds to accompany the meaning of your words."

April decided we didn't need to do it again, which pleased me no end. We both sprawled out under the umbrella and rested. It was as hot as Hades, but we were surviving it together. That made all the difference. April announced that we were done, and I was not about to argue.

We smoked and talked about our dreams for our future companies. We discussed eventually opening a nonprofit organization to create scholarships and to help pay for alarms at underprivileged schools. And she began to describe the next invention she wanted to start on, which she had been considering for years. She told me that if I told anyone, then she'd have to kill me. We laughed and sweated and enjoyed the moment.

We trudged back across the street to our little Lantana home. I stopped and watched April disappear into the house. I considered how long I had known her and all she'd driven me to do. We had met exactly four months previously. I was astounded that it was only that long. We were 90 percent done on my book; April had filed for the patent on our life-saving alarm; I had just shot a video for the Internet. I could hear April singing a Teri Catlin song from inside the house. I took a huge, healthy breath, spread my arms wide, looked up to the sun, and smiled. I was on top of the mountain.

What a painful, frightening, lifelong whirlwind I had been living in.

I'd survived hell over and over. I'd stood back up repeatedly. I was knocked down, and I came up swinging more times than I could count. I was a survivor and was finally proud of myself. April had taught me to trust myself and what I was doing. I had re-met my family on my own terms and was happy with their response. I had survived the toils of my lifetime and was about to embark on the most serious journey of all.

I could now say with firm belief that I was an advocate for children. I was going to make a huge difference in people's lives, and I knew it. Our company would provide the change needed for parents to be confident that their babies would be safe.

I am Kathryn Harriet Muhammad, mutt extraordinaire, and I know without a shadow of a doubt that I have arrived at my seat in history, with triumph!

Photos

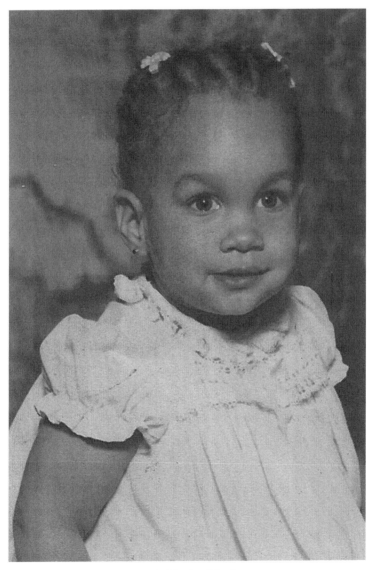

Beautiful baby Kathryn

A precocious Kathryn (center) and her cousin Tanesha (far left)

A happy Kathryn at the age of 7

Kathryn toting her cousin

Kathryn and Lawrence Muhammad in her last childhood picture with her father.

Kathryn happy on her tainted vacation

Kathryn's last picture at New Delray

Kathryn pleads her case at the Early Learning Coalition meeting

Kathryn praying for the life of her company at the Early Learning
Coalition meeting

An emaciated Kathryn and her Lawyer Betty Resch at the Florida
Department of Health

Vito, April and Vincent

April, Kathryn and Teri Catlin at the Improv

Made in the USA
Charleston, SC
24 January 2013